THE NEW HARTFORD MEMORIAL LIBRARY

D0811577

Harrods

BOOK OF
CAKES & DESSERTS

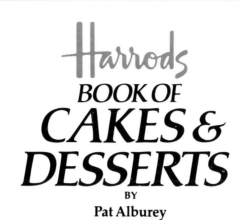

Harrods
BOOK OF
CAKES &
DESSERTS

BY

Pat Alburey

EBURY PRESS
LONDON

Published by Ebury Press
Division of The National Magazine Company Ltd
Colquhoun House
27–37 Broadwick Street
London W1V 1FR

First Impression 1986

ISBN 0 85223 577 1

Text copyright © 1986 by The National Magazine Company Ltd
Photographs copyright © 1986 by The National Magazine Company Ltd
All rights reserved. No Part of this publication may be reproduced,
stored in a retrieval system, or transmitted in any form or by
any means, electronic, mechanical, photocopying, recording, or
otherwise, without the prior permission of the copyright owner.

EDITORS: Fiona MacIntyre and Felicity Jackson
ART DIRECTOR: Frank Phillips
DESIGNER: Marshall Art
PHOTOGRAPHY: Grant Symon
STYLIST: Sue Russell
HOME ECONOMISTS: Susanna Tee, Janet Smith and Maxine Clark

Ebury Press would like to thank Harrods, and their archivist
Margaret Baber, for allowing the use of the black and white
illustrations taken from Harrods catalogues.

Computerset by MFK Typesetting Ltd, Hitchin, Herts
Printed and bound in Italy by New Interlitho Spa, Milan

Contents

6
INTRODUCTION

8
CAKES AND PASTRIES

31
FRESH FRUIT DESSERTS

46
TARTS AND PIES

56
HOT SOUFFLÉS

64
CREAMS, MOUSSES AND COLD SOUFFLÉS

76
MERINGUES

86
BASIC RECIPES

95
INDEX

*All eggs used in this book are size 2
unless otherwise stated.*

Introduction

HOWEVER splendid the previous courses may have been, it is, without doubt, the dessert that creates the most impression and is the course most eagerly awaited. Its choice must be considered with great deliberation, so as not to disappoint those who eagerly await its arrival. But it must be chosen to complement the rest of the meal, not to take all the applause.

Cooking is all about tempting and pleasing the appetite, and the most important factor to remember when choosing a dessert is that it is served at the end of the meal, when appetites are waning. With a few exceptions, a dessert does not have an aroma to help stimulate the appetite, it relies purely on the visual senses.

Presentation is everything – desserts must look as exquisite as possible, so that in delighting the eye, the appetite will be tempted. But it must not be too elaborate, or the thought of eating it may be overwhelming. A softly frozen sorbet, elegantly served, can have as much impact, and be even more welcome, than an elaborate pastry creation lavishly decorated with cream. It all depends on what has gone before.

The dessert should complement the main courses in both flavour and colour, and provide a

contrast in texture. Don't serve a pie followed by a pastry dessert. Main courses consisting of soft textures should be followed by a dessert with a crisp or crunchy texture. Pancakes after pasta would be wrong, a fresh salad, or light meringue gateau would be better.

The dessert should not contain any distinctive ingredient used in the previous courses. When main courses contain a lot of cream, avoid using it for the dessert. Follow creamy or spicy foods with a more sharply flavoured dessert.

Always consider the occasion and be wary of mingling elaborate dishes with homely ones. A plain omelette and salad would be best followed by something like an apple pie, but that same pie served as the climax to a celebration dinner for 12 would look very out of place; a beautifully moulded bavarois would be more fitting for a formal occassion..

Colours should complement each other; a colourful meal is usually a more interesting one, though it is now quite fashionable to chose a single colour theme, such as white or green for the whole meal.

Hot desserts are always appreciated more in the winter than in the summer, but even a cold summer lunch would benefit from a light hot dessert such as a soufflé, or flambéed apples; hot fruit pies can be warming without being heavy. Cold desserts are very acceptable in summer or winter, particularly when they follow heavier main courses. They also have the advantage of needing little or no last minute attention.

Serve a cheese platter before the dessert to stimulate the appetite and enable the last drop of wine to be drunk before the dessert. Once the palate has savoured something sweet, wine will seem very sour tasting, unless it is a sweet one such as a sauterne.

These are the guidelines, but the final choice is, of course a personal one.

Cakes and Pastries

IN EUROPE, cakes have their origins long before Christian times, when disc-shaped cakes were made to celebrate the Midsummer Solstice, their round shape being like the sun. For centuries since Christian times, cakes have been baked for symbolic reasons to celebrate important days in the Christian calendar, with every country having its own specialities. The French celebrate the feast of Epiphany by baking a simple flat round cake called a Galette, or Twelfth Night Cake. It is from these simple beginnings that more elaborate cakes have developed.

No birthday, christening, or marriage would be complete without a special cake being made to celebrate the occasion, the cake nearly always being the centre-piece of the buffet table. In Germany, a birthday is celebrated with a family gathering, seated around a table laden with torte. They remain seated for hours, eating cake and drinking coffee, and a few schnaps too! Cakes have long been associated with conviviality, happy times and friendship. They are always made for sharing with others.

All over western Europe one can see konditorei and pâtisseries displaying torte, or gâteaux, that are second to none anywhere in the world. Austria and Germany are particularly famous for their torte, the most famous being Vienna's Sachertorte, which was invented by Franz Sacher to satisfy the sweet tooth of Prince Klemens von Metternich, a famous statesman. From the Black Forest, Germany has given us Schwarzwalder Kirschtorte, a rich chocolate cake made with Morello cherries and cherry liqueur.

France is famous for its pastry gâteaux, the lightest and richest ones being made with choux pastry. The larger, elaborate sponge gâteaux with mousse-like fillings are peculiar to Austria and Germany. The famous named gâteaux are just the tip of the iceberg; all over Europe there are thousands more, sadly, known only to a privileged few.

Coffee and cake, are a way of life to the Austrians, Germans and Swiss. Every coffee house has its own array of beautiful torte. They are meeting houses for friends and families, particularly on a Sunday afternoon, where they can linger over a coffee and a huge slice of torte, usually topped with whipped cream, to gossip and to exchange their news.

PISTACHIO AND HAZELNUT GALETTE (page 16)

Linzertorte

Linzertorte, another Austrian speciality, is really more of a jam tart than a gâteau. However one classifies Linzertorte, it is a delicious and quickly made cake. The pastry acquires its distinctive colouring from the fact that the almonds are ground with their skins on. Linzertorte is best eaten when it has cooled to room temperature, but is still excellent cold.

225 g (8 oz) plain flour
175 g (6 oz) unblanched
  almonds, ground finely
pinch of salt
5 ml (1 tsp) freshly
  ground cinnamon
100 g (4 oz) icing sugar,
  sifted
finely grated rind of
  1 lemon
225 g (8 oz) unsalted
  butter, at room
  temperature
2 large egg yolks
350 g (12 oz) raspberry
  conserve

Glaze
1 small egg, beaten with
  15 ml (1 tbsp) milk
5 ml (1 tsp) caster sugar

Decoration
15 g (½ oz) flaked
  almonds, optional
icing sugar for sifting

SERVES TWELVE TO SIXTEEN

Mix the flour, almonds, salt, cinnamon, icing sugar and lemon rind in a bowl. Cut the butter into pieces and add to the mixture with the egg yolks. Work all the ingredients together until they form a smooth ball of pastry. Wrap in clingfilm and chill for about 40 minutes, until the pastry is firm.

Place a square of aluminium foil on a baking sheet, then place a 28 cm (11 inch) 3 cm (1¼ inch) deep, flan ring in the centre. Butter the ring, then bring the aluminium foil up smoothly around the side of the ring to seal the bottom edge and prevent the pastry seeping out at the beginning of baking.

Roll out just a little more than half of the pastry on a lightly floured surface to a round 2.5 cm (1 inch) larger than the flan ring. Line the flan ring with the pastry, pressing it smoothly around the side. Trim the pastry level with the top of the flan ring.

Add the pastry trimmings to the remaining pastry and roll out to an oblong about 28 cm×15 cm (11×6 inches), the same thickness as the pastry in the flan ring. Trim the edges neatly, then cut into 10 long strips, about 1 cm (½ inch) wide.

Spread the raspberry conserve evenly over the bottom of the pastry in the flan ring. Lay the pastry strips flat, on top of the jam (the sides of the pastry will be above them) in a lattice pattern, cutting them to fit exactly. Loosen the sides of the pastry from the flan ring with a small palette knife, then bring them down over the pastry strips to form a neat border.

Lightly whisk the egg, milk, and sugar for the glaze together, then brush evenly over the pastry. Sprinkle the torte with flaked almonds, if wished. Bake at 220°C (400°F) mark 6 for 10 minutes, then reduce the oven temperature to 180°C (350°F) mark 4 and continue cooking for 35 minutes until the pastry is golden brown. Allow to cool on the baking sheet without removing the flan ring.

When the pastry begins to firm up, run a palette knife carefully around the sides to loosen the flan ring – but do not remove the ring until the torte has cooled to room temperature.

Remove the flan ring, sift the icing sugar over the torte and transfer to a doily-lined plate.

Pithiviers

This decorative puff pastry cake is a speciality of Pithiviers, a town just south of Paris. It is filled with a rum-flavoured almond cream, and the top is scored in a distinctive spiral pattern.

---

1 quantity of puff pastry (see page 89)	100 g (4 oz) ground almonds
Filling	*Glaze*
50 g (2 oz) unsalted butter	1 egg
100 g (4 oz) icing sugar, sifted	10 ml (2 tsp) icing sugar, sifted
2 egg yolks	
30 ml (2 tbsp) rum	MAKES EIGHT SLICES

Cut the pastry into two equal pieces. Roll out each piece on a lightly floured surface to a square, a little larger than 25 cm (10 inches). Cut a 25 cm (10 inch) round from each piece of pastry, using a large plate or saucepan lid as a guide. Place one of the rounds on a baking sheet.

Beat the butter until very soft, then beat in the icing sugar, egg yolks and rum. Mix in the ground almonds until well combined.

Spread the almond filling in the centre of the pastry round on the baking sheet, leaving a border of about 2.5 cm (1 inch) all round. Brush the pastry border with a little cold water, then place the second pastry round on top to enclose the filling. Press the edges firmly together to seal. Chill the pastry for at least 30 minutes.

Make the glaze by lightly beating the egg and the icing sugar together. Lightly flake the edge of the pastry by tapping it gently with a small knife, then decorate the edge by fluting it all the way round with the back of a knife.

Brush the top of the pastry with beaten egg glaze – do not allow the glaze to run down the side of the pastry as this will prevent it rising evenly. Using a small sharp knife, mark the top of the pastry with long curved lines, scoring about halfway through the pastry, starting at the centre of the pastry and ending at the edge. The lines should be about 0.5 cm (¼ inch) apart and should look like a spiral pattern when finished. Make a small hole in the centre to allow the steam to escape.

Bake at 230°C (450°F) mark 8 for about 20–25 minutes until well risen and golden brown. Remove from the oven and cool on the baking sheet. Serve when the pastry has cooled to room temperature.

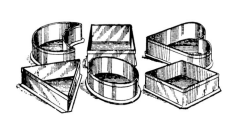

Chocolate Eclairs

Most of the eclairs sold in pâtisseries in France are filled with crème pâtissière, either vanilla, chocolate, or coffee flavoured and are iced with chocolate or fondant icing. They may also be glazed with caramel.

1 quantity of choux pastry (see page 91)	*Icing*
1 quantity of crème pâtissière (see page 93) with 65 g (2½ oz) plain chocolate melted with the milk	100 g (4 oz) plain chocolate, broken into small pieces
	30 ml (2 tbsp) water
	25 g (1 oz) unsalted butter
	MAKES TWENTY-TWO

Line two large baking sheets with non-stick baking paper cutting it to fit neatly.

Put the choux pastry into a piping bag fitted with a 1 cm (½ inch) plain nozzle. Pipe the choux pastry on to the lined baking sheets in short straight lines, 9 cm (3½ inches) long, cutting the choux pastry cleanly away from the nozzle at the end of each line with a small knife. Bake at 220°C (425°F) mark 7 for 25–30 minutes until well risen, golden brown and crisp. Remove from the oven and pierce each eclair at one end to allow the steam to escape. Return to the oven for 5 minutes to dry out completely. Transfer to a wire rack to cool.

Put the crème pâtissière into a piping bag fitted with a 0.5 cm (¼ inch) plain nozzle and pipe the cream into each eclair through the hole made in the end, as you pipe the cream into the eclairs, shake them gently to make sure that the cream goes right to the bottom.

To make the icing, put the chocolate in a deep plate with the water. Place the plate over a saucepan of hot water until the chocolate melts, stirring until smooth. Remove from the heat and gradually stir in the butter.

Dip the top of each eclair in the chocolate, then place on a wire rack and put in a cool place until set.

Mille-Feuille

Translated, mille-feuille means a thousand leaves. Mille-feuille is made up of layers of puff pastry sandwiched together with crème pâtissière. Classic mille-feuille is made up of round layers of pastry, but it can also be made with oblong layers, which are easier to handle.

1 quantity of puff pastry (see page 89)	30 ml (2 tbsp) boiling water
1 quantity of crème pâtissière (see page 93)	40 g (1½ oz) almonds, blanched, toasted and finely chopped
45 ml (3 tbsp) raspberry conserve	
175 g (6 oz) icing sugar, sifted	MAKES EIGHT SLICES

Roll out the puff pastry on a lightly floured surface to an oblong, 33×37.5 cm (13×15 inches). Trim the pastry edges neatly, then prick the pastry well with a fork. Cut into three oblongs, each one 12.5×33 cm (5×13 inches). Place the pastry strips on baking sheets and chill for 30 minutes.

Dampen the baking sheets around the pastry strips with a little cold water. Bake at 230°C (450°F) mark 8 for 25–30 minutes until well risen and golden brown. Cool the pastry strips on a wire rack.

Place the puff pastry layers, one on top of the

other and trim the sides neatly. Choose the most even layer for the top, turning it upside down if necessary to make a flat surface.

Place the bottom layer on a serving dish and spread with half of the crème pâtissière and jam. Place the second pastry layer on top and spread with the remaining jam and crème pâtissière, then place the last layer of pastry on top with the flat side uppermost.

Mix the icing sugar with the hot water to form an icing thick enough to coat the back of the spoon – do not make it too thin. Spread the icing evenly over the top layer of pastry and immediately sprinkle it with the chopped almonds. Allow the icing to set. Serve cut into slices.

Religieuse

Two-tiered choux puffs, which acquired their name from the fact that they look like nuns. These are filled with a coffee-flavoured crème pâtissière, and iced with a coffee glacé icing. They may also be filled with cream and coated with chocolate icing, if preferred.

---

1 quantity of choux pastry (see page 91)
1½ quantities of crème pâtissière (see page 93) with 15 ml (1 tbsp) coffee granules added to the milk when making the custard
½ quantity of crème Chantilly (see page 94)

Icing
225 g (8 oz) icing sugar, sifted
5 ml (1 tsp) coffee granules
45 ml (3 tbsp) boiling water

MAKES TWELVE

Line several baking sheets with non-stick baking paper. Put the choux pastry into a piping bag fitted with a 1 cm (½ inch) plain nozzle. Pipe 12 buns, 5 cm (2 inches) in diameter, on to the baking sheets, spacing them well apart. Then pipe another 12 smaller buns, about 4 cm (1½ inches) in diameter. Bake the buns, with the small ones placed below the larger ones, at 220°C (425°F) mark 7 for about 35 minutes until they are well risen, golden brown and crisp. Remove from the oven and pierce underneath to allow the steam to escape. Return the buns to the oven for 5 minutes to dry out completely. Transfer to a wire rack to cool.

Put the coffee-flavoured crème pâtissière into a piping bag fitted with a 0.5 cm (¼ inch) plain nozzle. Fill all the buns with the crème pâtissière, piping it in through the hole made in the bottom. Place the buns, spaced well apart, on a wire rack. Place the rack over a tray or large plate.

To make the icing, put the icing sugar into a bowl and make a well in the centre. Dissolve the coffee granules in the boiling water, then add to the icing sugar and mix together to form a smooth, shiny icing that will coat the back of the spoon. Spoon the icing evenly over each choux bun, then leave until completely set before fitting together.

Whip the crème Chantilly until thick enough to pipe, then fill a piping bag fitted with a large star nozzle. Pipe a rosette on top of each large choux bun, then carefully place the smaller buns on top of the cream, pressing gently into the cream to secure.

Schwarzwalder Kirschtorte
(Black Forest Cherry Cake)

This famous, and much loved, cake from the Black Forest is perfect for any grand occasion, or as a dessert for a dinner party. The cherries should really be fresh Morello cherries, but as these are not always easy to come by, canned cherries can be used instead. When fresh Morello cherries are available, poach them in a sugar syrup and remove their stones. The following recipe is a very lavish version.

Chocolate Génoise
7 eggs
200 g (7 oz) caster sugar
100 g (4 oz) plain flour
75 g (3 oz) cocoa
90 g (3½ oz) unsalted
   butter, melted and
   cooled

Filling
two 454 g (16 oz) cans
   pitted dark cherries
200 g (7 oz) caster sugar
105 ml (7 tbsp) Kirsch

1 litre (1¾ pints) double
   cream
30 ml (2 tbsp) icing sugar,
   sifted

Decoration
175 g (6 oz) plain
   chocolate at room
   temperature
12 fresh cherries with
   stalks, or maraschino
   cherries

MAKES TWELVE SLICES

Make the chocolate Génoise as instructed on page 86, sifting the flour and cocoa together twice before adding to the egg mixture. Bake the sponge cake at 180°C (350°F) mark 4 for 35–40 minutes.

Make the chocolate decoration. Line a baking sheet with greaseproof paper, then working directly over the paper, pull a potato peeler along the edge of the chocolate, not the flat surface, to form a curl.

Continue until the chocolate is used up. Chill the chocolate curls until needed.

Make the filling, drain the cherries, reserving 300 ml (½ pint) of their juice. Put the cherry juice into a saucepan with the caster sugar. Heat gently until the sugar dissolves, then boil the syrup until it reduces by about half and is thickened. Allow to cool, then stir in 45 ml (3 tbsp) Kirsch. Whip half of the cream with 30 ml (2 tbsp) Kirsch and 15 ml (1 tbsp) icing sugar.

Cut the chocolate sponge into three layers. Cut a piece of card the same size as the sponge cake. Place the card on the work surface, then place the bottom layer of sponge on the card. Fit a torten ring around the sponge cake, snugly but not too tightly. Or, cut a strip of thin card long enough to fit around the sponge cake and 6 cm (2½ inches deep). Secure the card firmly in position with sticky tape.

Brush the cherry syrup all over the layer of sponge cake to moisten it well. Spread with half the whipped cream, then arrange half the cherries on top. Place the second layer of sponge cake on top of the cherries, and moisten well with more cherry syrup. Spread with the remaining whipped cream, and cover with the remaining cherries. Brush the underside of the top layer of sponge with cherry syrup and place it, syrup-side down, on top of the cherries. Press the gâteau firmly together.

Whip the remaining cream with the remaining Kirsch and icing sugar. Spread a layer of cream over the top of the gâteau. Remove the torten ring, or the card, from around the gâteau.

Spread the side of the gâteau with a smooth layer of cream, then coat the sides evenly with the chocolate curls – the piece of card under the gâteau will make it easy to pick the gâteau up for this process.

Place the gâteau on a serving plate, and mark the top into 12 equal sections. Whip the remaining cream until it is thick enough to pipe, then fill a piping bag fitted with a medium-sized star nozzle.

Working from the centre of the gâteau out, pipe a large shell of cream in each section on top of the gâteau, then pipe a star of cream where each shell finishes, sprinkle any remaining chocolate curls over the top of the gâteau, then, decorate the stars with the fresh or maraschino cherries. Keep the gâteau in a cool place until ready to serve.

Paris-Brest

This speciality of Paris is a large choux ring, split and filled with praline-flavoured cream. It could also be filled with crème Chantilly and fresh fruits, such as strawberries and raspberries. The top is strewn with slivered almonds, giving it a very attractive appearance.

1 quantity of choux pastry (see page 91)	100 g (4 oz) caster sugar
25 g (1 oz) almonds, blanched and cut into fine slivers	8 sponge fingers
	45–60 ml (3–4 tbsp) Grand Marnier
	600 ml (1 pint) double cream
Filling	icing sugar for sifting
100 g (4 oz) unblanched almonds	SERVES EIGHT TO TEN

Line a large baking sheet with non-stick baking paper, then draw a 20.5 cm (8 inch) circle on the paper, using a plate as a guide.

Put the choux pastry into a large piping bag fitted with a large star nozzle. Following the drawn circle, pipe two rings of choux closely together on the baking sheet, then pipe two more rings on the top. Scatter the slivered almonds evenly over the top, then bake at 220°C (425°F) mark 7 for 40–45 minutes until well risen and crispy. Remove the choux ring from the oven and pierce it in several places to allow the steam to escape. Return to the oven for 5–10 minutes to dry out completely.

Transfer the choux ring to a wire rack and allow to cool for a few minutes, then slice horizontally into two, cutting evenly around the centre. Separate the two halves, then scoop out any uncooked pastry from the centre. Allow to cool completely.

To make the filling, put the unblanched almonds and sugar into a heavy-based saucepan and heat very gently until the sugar dissolves and turns a rich caramel colour – do not let it become too dark as this will make the praline bitter. Pour the nuts on to a lightly oiled baking sheet, allow to cool, then finely crush or grind.

Cut the sponge fingers in half and lay them in a shallow dish. Sprinkle the Grand Marnier over them, cover and leave to stand until the sponge fingers have absorbed the liqueur.

Whip the cream until it just holds its shape, then carefully fold in the praline.

Place the bottom half of the choux ring on a plate and fill with half the praline cream. Break up the soaked sponge fingers with a fork, then spoon over the praline cream. Spread the remaining praline cream evenly on top of the sponge fingers. Replace the top of the choux ring, then sift lightly with icing sugar. Chill until ready to serve.

Pistachio and Hazelnut Galette

This simple cake is made with two rounds of pistachio and hazelnut pastry, filled with a Grand Marnier-flavoured cream, mangoes and mandarin orange segments.

200 g (7 oz) plain flour
pinch of salt
50 g (2 oz) icing sugar
50 g (2 oz) pistachio nuts, skinned and ground fairly finely
25 g (1 oz) hazelnuts, skinned, toasted, and ground fairly finely
200 g (7 oz) unsalted butter, cut into pieces

Filling
600 ml (1 pint) double cream

finely grated rind of 1 orange
30 ml (2 tbsp) Grand Marnier
15 ml (1 tbsp) icing sugar
1 large ripe mango
425 g (15 oz) can mandarin orange segments
icing sugar for sifting
chopped pistachio nuts for sprinkling

MAKES TWELVE SLICES

Sift the flour, salt and icing sugar into a bowl, add the nuts and mix well together. Rub the butter into the flour and nut mixture, working the ingredients together gently until they form a ball.

Cut the pastry into two equal pieces, roll out each piece on a lightly floured surface to a round a little smaller than 25 cm (10 inches). Place each pastry round in a 25 cm (10 inch) fluted flan tin, then press the pastry gently over the base of the tins until it fits exactly – smooth the pastry with the back of a spoon, but do not stretch it.

Prick with a fork, and bake at 180°C (350°F) mark 4 for 30–35 minutes until the pastry is cooked and very lightly browned (if you have only one flan tin, bake the pastry rounds one at a time, keeping the one not being baked refrigerated until needed). Remove the cooked pastry rounds from the oven and immediately cut one of the rounds into 12 triangle-shaped pieces. Allow to cool slightly, then transfer to wire racks to cool completely.

Whip the cream with the orange rind, Grand Marnier and icing sugar until it will hold soft peaks. Peel the mango, then cut the flesh from the stone in long thin slices. Drain the orange segments well, putting about 12 of the best ones aside for decoration.

Carefully place the whole pastry round on a large plate. Spread a generous layer of cream over the pastry, then arrange the mango slices and orange segments evenly over the cream.

Whip remaining cream until thick enough to pipe and fill a piping bag fitted with a large star nozzle. Pipe 12 large rosettes on top of the fruits, about 2.5 cm (1 inch) in from the edge. Arrange the triangle-shaped pieces of pastry on top of the gâteau, placing them at an angle, each one supported by a rosette of cream. Sift icing sugar lightly over the gateau. Decorate the gâteau with the remaining cream and reserved mandarin orange segments and sprinkle over the nuts.

GÂTEAU SAINT-HONORÉ (page 18)

Jalousie

A simple puff pastry cake filled with raspberry conserve, perfect for afternoon tea, or to have with coffee.

1 quantity of puff pastry (see page 89)	1 small egg, beaten with 10 ml (2 tsp) sifted icing sugar
225 g (8 oz) raspberry conserve	icing sugar for sifting

MAKES EIGHT SLICES

Roll out the puff pastry on a lightly floured surface to a square a little larger than 30 cm (12 inches). Trim the pastry edges to form an exact 30 cm (12 inch) square. Cut the pastry equally in half. Place the pastry lengths on baking sheets and chill for about 10 minutes. Chilling the pastry at this stage will make it much easier to assemble.

Spread the raspberry conserve down the centre of one of the pieces of pastry, leaving a 2.5 cm (1 inch) border all round.

Remove the second piece of pastry from the baking sheet and fold in half lengthways, then make cuts all along the folded edge to within 2.5 cm (1 inch) of the edges, spacing the cuts about 1 cm (½ inch) apart. Without unfolding the pastry, place it on top of the pastry spread with jam so that the edges line up with the bottom piece of pastry, then carefully unfold the pastry to cover the jam completely. Press all the pastry edges well together to seal. Chill for 30 minutes.

Remove the chilled jalousie from the refrigerator, then flake the edge with a small knife and mark into flutes. Brush the top with the beaten egg – do not allow the glaze to run down the sides as it will prevent them from rising. Bake at 230°C (450°F) mark 8 for 20–30 minutes until it is well risen, and golden brown. Allow to cool. Sift with icing sugar then place on a doily-lined tray. To serve, cut into slices across the jalousie.

Gâteau Saint-Honoré

This gâteau is named after Saint-Honoré, who was a Bishop of Amiens and is considered the patron saint of bakers. It is a wonderful gâteau, that combines two types of pastry, pâte sucrée and choux, to form a case that may be filled with an endless variety of fillings. This recipe uses the traditional crème Saint-Honoré, topped with a chocolate-flavoured cream.

1 quantity of pâte sucrée (see page 92)	*Caramel* 225 g (8 oz) granulated sugar
1 quantity of choux pastry (see page 91)	75 ml (3 fl oz) water
Crème Saint-Honoré double quantity of ingredients for crème pâtissière (see page 93)	*Topping* 75 g (3 oz) plain chocolate, broken into small pieces
15 ml (1 tbsp) powdered gelatine	45 ml (3 tbsp) water
45 ml (3 tbsp) water	300 ml (½ pint) double cream
30 ml (2 tbsp) Grand Marnier	chopped pistachio nuts for sprinkling

SERVES TWELVE

Roll out the pâte sucrèe on a flat, or upturned, baking sheet to a round a little larger than 28 cm (11 inches) in diameter. Using a flan ring or saucepan lid as a guide, cut the pastry into a 28 cm (11 inch) round. Remove the trimmings, then prick the pastry all over with a fork. Chill for 30 minutes.

Put the choux pastry into a piping bag fitted with a 1 cm (½ inch) plain nozzle. Pipe a single ring of choux pastry around the edge of the pâte sucrèe, about 0.5 cm (¼ inch) in from the edge. Bake at 200°C (400°F) mark 6 for 25–30 minutes until the choux pastry is well risen, golden brown and crisp. Remove from the oven and pierce the choux ring at intervals to allow the steam to escape. Return to the oven for 2–3 minutes to dry out completely. Transfer to a wire rack to cool.

Meanwhile, line a large baking sheet with non-stick baking paper and pipe the remaining choux pastry in whirls, about 4 cm (1½ inches) in diameter, on the baking sheet, spacing them well apart (only 14–15 buns are needed for the gâteau but it is best to make extra buns because all those used have to be perfect). Bake at 220°C (425°F) mark 7, for 25–30 minutes until well risen, golden brown and crisp. Remove from the oven and pierce each bun underneath to allow the steam to escape. Return to the oven for about 5 minutes to dry out completely. Transfer to a wire rack to cool.

To make the crème Saint-Honoré, prepare the crème pâtissière to the stage where the custard is cooled, ready for adding the egg whites and cream. Sprinkle the gelatine over the water in a small bowl and leave to soak for 2 minutes. Stand in a small pan of hot water, stirring until dissolved and quite hot. Whisk the egg whites until stiff, then fold into the cooled custard. Whip the cream, adding the Grand Marnier, until it just holds its shape, then quickly whisk in the gelatine. Fold the cream into the custard. Keep at room temperature while completing the gâteau.

Spoon some of the crème Saint-Honoré into a piping bag fitted with a 0.5 cm (¼ inch) plain nozzle, and fill 14–15 of the best choux buns, piping it in through the hole made in the bottom. Scrape any cream from the base of the buns with a small palette knife. Put the buns aside while making the caramel.

To make the caramel, put the sugar into a saucepan with the water heat gently until the sugar has dissolved, brushing down the sides of the saucepan with the hot water from time to time. Bring the syrup to the boil and boil until it turns a golden caramel colour. Immediately, plunge the base of the saucepan into cold water to prevent the caramel darkening further. Place the saucepan in a large bowl and fill the bowl to halfway up the side of the saucepan with boiling water – this will keep the caramel fluid.

Place the pâte sucrée base on a plate. Take one of the choux buns and dip the base in the caramel, then place it on the choux ring, holding it in position for a few seconds to secure. Continue with the remaining buns, placing them close together. Spoon the remaining caramel over each bun to coat evenly. Spoon the remaining crème Saint-Honoré into the choux case. Chill while making the topping.

Put the chocolate into a small bowl with the water. Place the bowl over a pan of hot water until the chocolate melts, stirring frequently until smooth. Remove from the heat and allow to cool. Whip the cream until thick but not buttery, then carefully fold in the cooled chocolate.

Put the chocolate cream into a piping bag fitted with a medium-sized star nozzle and pipe the cream decoratively over the top of a the crème Saint-Honoré. Sprinkle with pistachio nuts and serve. If not serving immediately, keep in a cool place – the gâteau will stand quite well for 1–2 hours.

Raspberry Torte

This rich, creamy cake is very like the many elaborate gâteaux one finds across Europe – they don't have famous names, but are the proud creations of individual cafés and pâtisseries. This one is made with a raspberry-flavoured bavarois mixture, generously decorated with cream and fresh raspberries.

Génoise
4 eggs
100 g (4 oz) caster sugar
100 g (4 oz) plain flour, sifted
50 g (2 oz) unsalted butter, melted and cooled

Pastry base
1 quantity of pâte sucrée (see page 92)
15 ml (1 tbsp) sieved raspberry conserve

Bavarois
20 ml (4 tsp) powdered gelatine
45 ml (3 tbsp) water
4 egg yolks
25 g (1 oz) caster sugar
225 ml (8 fl oz) milk
300 ml (½ pint) double cream
30 ml (2 tbsp) icing sugar, sifted
225 g (8 oz) fresh raspberries, sieved

Topping
7.5 ml (1½ tsp) powdered gelatine
30 ml (2 tbsp) water
300 ml (½ pint) double cream
15 ml (1 tbsp) icing sugar, sifted
15 ml (1 tbsp) Kirsch

Decoration
300 ml (½ pint) double cream
50 g (2 oz) flaked almonds, lightly toasted
fresh raspberries for decoration

MAKES TWELVE SLICES

Make the Génoise as instructed on page 86.

Roll the pâte sucrée out on a flat, or upturned baking sheet to a round a little larger than 25 cm (10 inches). Cut the pastry to a neat 25 cm (10 inch) round, using a large plate as a guide. Remove the trimmings, then prick the pastry well all over with a fork. Chill for 30 minutes, then bake at 220°C (425°F) mark 7 for 20–25 minutes until very lightly browned.

To make the raspberry bavarois, sprinkle the gelatine over the water in a small bowl and leave to soak for 2 minutes. Lightly whisk the egg yolks and the caster sugar together. Heat the milk until almost boiling, then whisk it into the egg yolks. Cook over a pan of hot water until the custard is thick enough to coat the back of the spoon evenly (or, cook in a microwave oven on full power, for 2–2½ minutes, stirring every 30 seconds with a wire whisk).

Immediately the custard thickens, pour it through a nylon sieve into a clean bowl. Add the gelatine and stir until dissolved. Cool, stirring frequently.

Whip the double cream with the icing sugar until it will hold soft peaks. Mix the cooked custard and the raspberry purée together until well blended, then fold in the cream. Cut the sponge into two even-sized layers, trimming the top edge to level.

Place the pâte sucrée base on a plate, then spread evenly with the raspberry conserve. Place the bottom layer of sponge on top of the jam. Trim the pastry base to exactly the same size as the sponge. Place a torten ring around the pastry and sponge to fit snugly, but not too tightly. (If you do not have a torten ring – cut a length of flexible card long enough to fit around the pastry, and about 7.5 cm (3 inches) deep. Secure the card with sticky tape.

Pour the raspberry bavarois mixture on top of the sponge, then chill until beginning to set. Place the top layer of sponge on top and chill until very firm.

To make the topping, sprinkle the gelatine over the water in a small bowl and leave to soak for ☞

RASPBERRY TORTE (above)

2 minutes. Stand in a pan of hot water and stir until dissolved and hot. Whip the cream with the icing sugar and Kirsch until it will just hold its shape, then quickly whisk in the gelatine. Pour the cream over the top sponge and spread evenly. Chill until set.

To decorate, remove the torten ring or card. Whip the cream until it just holds its shape. Spread the sides of the torte with some of the cream, then coat evenly with flaked almonds. Whip the remaining cream until thick enough to pipe and fill a piping bag fitted with a medium-sized star nozzle.

Mark the top of the torte into 12. Starting at the outside edge and working to centre, pipe a curved scroll in each section. Decorate with raspberries.

Palmiers

A Parisian speciality, these pastries derive their name from their shape – the pastry is folded and cut in such a way that they look like hearts. These palmiers are filled with fresh strawberries and a strawberry cream, but they can be filled with crème Chantilly alone. As a special treat, use wild strawberries when they are available.

1 quantity of puff pastry (see page 89)	10 ml (2 tsp) icing sugar, sifted
100 g (4 oz) caster sugar	450 g (1 lb) fresh strawberries, hulled
10 ml (2 tsp) mixed ground spice	icing sugar for sifting
a little milk for brushing	
225 ml (8 fl oz) double cream	MAKES TEN
30 ml (2 tbsp) strawberry purée	

Roll out the puff pastry on a lightly floured surface to an oblong, about 48×53.5 cm (19×21 inches). Trim the edges neatly.

Mix the caster sugar and the ground spice together. Brush the pastry very lightly with a little milk, then sprinkle lightly with some of the sugar and spice. Fold the two longest sides to the centre of the pastry, to meet. Brush the pastry with a little more milk and sprinkle with more sugar and spice. Fold the long, folded sides, to the centre again. Brush the pastry with a little more milk and sprinkle with the remaining sugar and spice. Fold the two folded sides together.

Cut the pastry strip into twenty 2.5 cm (1 inch) wide pieces. Take one of the pastry pieces and turn it on to its side on a lightly floured surface, flatten slightly with the palm of your hand, then roll it out gently on a baking sheet to about 10 cm (4 inches) long, then repeat with the remaining pieces. Refrigerate the palmiers for about 30 minutes.

Brush each palmier with a little milk to glaze, then bake at 230°C (450°F) mark 8 for 20–25 minutes until they are golden brown and cooked. Transfer immediately to a wire rack to cool.

Whip the double cream with the strawberry purée and icing sugar until thick enough to pipe and fill a piping bag fitted with a large star nozzle. Pipe the cream on 10 of the pastry hearts. If the strawberries are very large, cut them into slices; if they are small, cut each one in half. Leave wild strawberries whole.

Arrange the strawberries on top of the cream, then place the remaining pastry hearts on top of the strawberries, placing them at a slight angle. Sift icing sugar lightly over the palmiers and serve.

Sachertorte

Famous the world over, Sachertorte was the invention of Franz Sacher, a master sugar baker, in Vienna in 1832. It is a very rich, moist, chocolate cake served, more often than not, with whipped cream. There are many versions of Sachertorte, some are made with an apricot jam filling, some are made without.

The traditional Sachertorte is covered with a chocolate fondant icing, but as this can be rather sweet, a ganach icing is used here. This icing is extremely simple to make and use. It sets with a high gloss, contrasting perfectly with the moist cake inside, both in texture and flavour. Sachertorte is not normally decorated, it looks superb in its simplicity.

---

175 g (6 oz) plain
  chocolate
175 g (6 oz) unsalted
  butter
100 g (4 oz) caster sugar
5 ml (1 tsp) vanilla
  essence
6 egg yolks
6 egg whites
175 g (6 oz) ground
  almonds
50 g (2 oz) potato flour

apricot glaze made with
  225 g (8 oz) apricot
  conserve (see page 94)

Icing
225 g (8 oz) plain
  chocolate, broken into
  small pieces
225 ml (8 fl oz) double
  cream

MAKES SIXTEEN SLICES

Thoroughly butter a 25 cm (10 inch) round springform tin, then line the bottom with non-stick baking paper. Lightly dust the sides with flour.

Break the chocolate into small pieces and put into a small bowl over a saucepan of hot water until the chocolate melts. Stir until smooth. Beat the butter with half the sugar and the vanilla essence until light and fluffy. Gradually beat in the egg yolks, and then the melted chocolate.

Whisk the egg whites until stiff, but not dry, then gradually whisk in the remaining caster sugar. Fold the egg whites into the chocolate mixture, alternately with the ground almonds and potato flour. Spoon the mixture into the prepared tin and bake at 180°C (350°F) mark 4 for 40–45 minutes, until a cocktail stick or wooden skewer inserted into the centre comes out clean. Allow the cake to cool in the tin.

Carefully remove the cake from the tin, turn it upside down and remove the baking paper and then slice the cake in half horizontally. Heat the apricot glaze until boiling. Place the bottom layer of cake on a wire rack. Spread apricot glaze all over the sponge layer, then place the second layer on top, pressing the two firmly together. Re-boil the apricot glaze and brush it evenly all over the cake until well coated. Allow to set. Place the cake on the rack over a large plate to ice it.

Make the icing, put the chocolate and cream into a pan and heat gently until the chocolate melts and blends smoothly with cream – do not allow to boil. Remove from the heat and stir gently to cool just a little. Pour the chocolate cream, all at once, into the centre of the cake and allow it to run over the top and down the sides to coat the cake completely. If necessary, ease the cream over the cake with a palette knife. Tap the rack gently to level the cream. Leave in a cool place, not the refrigerator, until the chocolate cream sets firmly. Serve the Sachertorte on a doily-lined plate.

Dobostorte

This cake, of Hungarian origination, is fascinating to make, but may be a little bewildering the first time you do so. It is made up of thin layers of fatless sponge mixture sandwiched together with chocolate butter cream. The top is glazed with caramel and the whole thing looks quite wonderful when completed. You don't need a special tin to bake it in, but you do need several baking sheets.

8 eggs	5 ml (1 tsp) vanilla
200 g (7 oz) caster sugar	essence
250 g (9 oz) plain flour,	65 g (2½ oz) cocoa, sifted
sifted	30 ml (2 tbsp) brandy,
	optional
Butter cream	
8 egg yolks	*Caramel*
350 g (12 oz) granulated	175 g (6 oz) granulated
sugar	sugar
150 ml (¼ pint) water	75 ml (5 tbsp) water
450 g (1 lb) unsalted	
butter	MAKES TWELVE SLICES

Cut six sheets of non-stick baking paper, about 28 cm (11 inches) square. Draw a 25 cm (10 inch) circle on each sheet of paper. Line as many baking sheets as you have with the paper. The sponge layers will have to be cooked in relays, depending on the number of shelves you have in your oven. It is a simple process to re-line the sheets.

To make the sponge layers, whisk the eggs and sugar in a bowl placed over a pan of hot water until pale and thick. Remove from the heat and continue whisking until cool, and the mixture holds the trail of a whisk. Gradually fold in the flour.

Put 30–45 ml (2–3 tbsp) of the mixture into the centre of the drawn circles, then spread evenly with a large palette knife to form thin layers. Bake the sponge layers, in batches, at 220° C (425° F) mark 7 for 6–7 minutes until they are lightly risen and firm to the touch. Remove from the oven and allow to cool.

To make the butter cream, whisk the egg yolks until very thick. Put the sugar into a saucepan with the water and heat gently until the sugar has dissolved, brushing down the sides of the pan with hot water. Boil the syrup until it reaches a temperature of 116° C (240° F) on a sugar thermometer, when a little of the syrup dropped into cold water forms a soft ball.

Whisk the syrup, in a thin stream, into the egg yolks. Continue to whisk until the mixture cools and thickens. Beat the butter until it is very light and fluffy, then beat in the vanilla, cocoa and brandy if using. Gradually beat the egg yolk mixture into the butter, a little at a time.

Carefully remove the sponge layers from the baking paper. Trim one of the sponges to form a neat round – cutting it to the largest round possible. Lightly butter a sheet of aluminium foil, then place the sponge layer on it. Thoroughly butter a large palette knife and a metal ruler.

To make the caramel, put the sugar into a pan with the water and heat gently until the sugar has dissolved, brushing down the sides of the pan. Boil the syrup until it turns a rich caramel colour – not too dark. Immediately, pour the caramel into the centre of the sponge cake on the aluminium foil, then spread it out evenly with the buttered palette knife. Working quite quickly, mark the caramel equally into 12 with the buttered ruler by pressing down gently but firmly on the caramel, and buttering the edge of the ruler each time you make an indentation. Allow the caramel to set.

Meanwhile, on a flat baking sheet, sandwich ☞

SORBETS (pages 34 and 35)

the remaining layers of sponge together, without trimming them, with generous layers of chocolate butter cream, ending with a layer of butter cream spread very evenly. Place the caramel coated layer of sponge on the top. Trim around the sides of the sponge layers, to level with the caramel coated layer.

Spread a good layer of butter cream around the sides of the torte, without letting it spoil the caramel coated layer, spreading it as smoothly as possible. Using a serrated cake scraper, mark the side of the torte with continuous lines – placing the torte on a turntable will make this job easier. Chill for about 30 minutes. Serve on a doily-lined plate. Cut into wedges by cutting through the caramel topping at the indentations.

Nusskuchen

Nusskuchen comes in many forms, but is always made with nuts of some kind. This is a light biscuit de Savoie sponge filled with a hazelnut butter cream.

1 biscuit de Savoie sponge cake (see page 87)	225 g (8 oz) unsalted butter
250 g (9 oz) hazelnuts	5 ml (1 tsp) vanilla essence
Butter cream	
4 egg whites	MAKES TWELVE SLICES
225 g (8 oz) icing sugar, sifted	

Make the biscuit de Savoie sponge as instructed and allow to cool.

Put the hazelnuts on to a baking sheet, then bake at 180°C (350°F) mark 4 for 10–15 minutes until their skins become loose. Put the nuts in a clean tea-towel and rub until the skins are removed. Put the skinned nuts on a baking sheet and return to the oven for 5–10 minutes until lightly browned. Remove from the oven and allow to cool. Put about 24 nuts aside for decoration, then chop the rest finely.

To make the butter cream, put the egg whites and icing sugar in a large bowl placed over a pan of hot water, then whisk until they form a stiff shiny meringue – do not allow the meringue to become too hot. Remove from the heat and continue whisking until the meringue is cooled, and will form stiff peaks.

Beat the butter until it is very light and fluffy, then beat in the vanilla essence. Gradually beat the meringue into the butter then divide the butter cream in two and mix half the chopped nuts into one half.

Slice the sponge cake horizontally into three even layers. Sandwich the sponge layers together with the hazelnut butter cream. Spread plain butter cream over the top and around the sides of the sponge cake. Coat the sides with the remaining chopped hazelnuts. Place the gâteau on a plate.

Put the remaining butter cream into a piping bag fitted with a small star nozzle. Pipe a decorative edge around the top of the gâteau, then decorate with the reserved whole hazelnuts. Keep in a cool place until ready to serve.

Danish Pastries

The Danes serve Danish pastries for breakfast, but they are perfect for serving with morning coffee, or afternoon tea. Serve freshly baked.

1 quantity of Danish
  pastry (see page 90)

Almond filling
25 g (1 oz) unsalted butter
50 g (2 oz) caster sugar
1 egg yolk
50 g (2 oz) ground
  almonds

Apricot filling
6 large ripe apricots,
  skinned, halved and
  stoned or, 12 canned
  apricot halves
5–10 ml (1–2 tsp) caster
  sugar

Spice filling
25 g (1 oz) butter
25 g (1 oz) caster sugar
5 ml (1 tsp) mixed ground
  spice
40 g (1½ oz) seedless
  raisins or currants

Glazes
1 egg, beaten
1 quantity of apricot glaze
  (see page 94)

Decorations
250 g (9 oz) icing sugar,
  sifted
lemon juice
25 g (1 oz) glacé cherries,
  chopped
25 g (1 oz) angelica,
  chopped
a little hot water
15 g (½ oz) pistachio nuts,
  skinned and chopped
15 ml (1 tbsp) rum
15 g (½ oz) flaked
  almonds, lightly
  toasted

MAKES EIGHTEEN

For almond crescents, make the almond filling by beating the butter with the caster sugar until soft, then beat in the egg yolk and ground almonds. Roll out one-third of the pastry on a lightly floured surface to a square, a little larger than 25 cm (10 inches). Cut a neat 25 cm (10 inch) round from the pastry, remove the trimmings, then cut the round into six triangles. Put one-quarter of the almond mixture aside and divide the rest into six.

Take one piece of dough, and place a piece of the almond mixture at the widest end. Roll the pastry up towards the point, then shape into a crescent. Place on a well greased baking sheet, with the point tucked under. Repeat with the remaining pastry, spacing the crescents well apart on the baking sheet.

For apricot envelopes, roll out one-third of the pastry to an oblong, 20.5×30 cm (8×12 inches). Trim the edges, then cut into six 10 cm (4 inch) squares. Place two apricot halves in the centre of each square, then place a small piece of the reserved almond mixture in each apricot. Sprinkle the apricots with sugar. Bring two opposite corners of the pastry to the centre, over the apricots, until they overlap slightly, moisten the joins with a little cold water to seal. Place well apart on a well greased baking sheet.

For spiced pinwheels, roll out the remaining pastry to an oblong 15×35 cm (6×14 inches). Beat the butter, sugar and spice together until soft and creamy, then spread it evenly over the pastry. Sprinkle the raisins evenly over the spice mixture. Roll the pastry up from a short end to form a wide roll. Cut the roll into six equal slices. Place the pinwheels, cut sides down, on a well greased baking sheet, spaced apart. Cover all the pastries loosely with clingfilm.

Leave the pastries in a warm place until they have doubled in size and are springy when pressed lightly with a fingertip. Brush the pastries with the beaten egg, then bake at 220°C (425°F) mark 7 for 15–20 minutes, until well risen, golden brown and crisp. Transfer to wire racks and glaze and decorate while hot. Boil the apricot glaze, then brush over all the pastries to glaze evenly.

To decorate crescents, mix 75 g (3 oz) of the icing sugar with sufficient lemon juice to form a thin icing, then dribble the icing over the hot pastries and sprinkle with the cherries and angelica. ☞

For apricot envelopes mix 75 g (3 oz) of the icing sugar with a little hot water to form a thin icing. Dribble the icing over the hot pastries and sprinkle with chopped pistachio nuts.

For pinwheels, mix the remaining icing sugar with the rum and just a little hot water to form a thin icing. Dribble the icing over the hot pastries and immediately sprinkle with the flaked almonds.

Rigo Jancsi

Absolute temptation! These rich squares of chocolate gâteau, classic in their make-up of chocolate flavoured Génoise and ganache were named after a gypsy violinist, who was said to have broken the heart of many a princess.

Chocolate Génoise	600 ml (1 pint) double
3 eggs	cream
75 g (3 oz) caster sugar	45 ml (3 tbsp) brandy
65 g (2½ oz) plain flour	
sifted with 15 g (½ oz)	*Icing*
cocoa	100 g (4 oz) plain
40 g (1½ oz) unsalted	chocolate, broken into
butter, melted and	small pieces
cooled	15 ml (1 tbsp) water
	30 ml (2 tbsp) brandy
Ganache	100 g (4 oz) icing sugar,
425 g (15 oz) plain	sifted
chocolate, broken into	
small pieces	MAKES TWENTY-FOUR
	SQUARES

Grease a 23×33 cm (9×13 inch) Swiss roll tin, with butter. Line the base with greaseproof paper. Make the Genoise as instructed on page 86 sifting the flour and cocoa together, then spread evenly in the prepared tin. Bake at 180°C (350°F) mark 4 for 20–25

minutes until the sponge is well risen, firm to the touch and beginning to shrink away from the sides of the tin. Allow the sponge to cool in the tin.

To make the ganache, put the chocolate and the cream into a large saucepan and heat gently, stirring, until the chocolate melts and blends smoothly with the cream, without letting the mixture boil. Pour the ganache into a bowl and allow to cool until quite cold, but not set hard, stirring the cream frequently to prevent a skin forming. When cold, whip the cream with the brandy until it is very light and fluffy, taking care not to overwhip.

Cut the chocolate sponge into two equal pieces, cutting across the width. Place one piece on a flat board or baking sheet. Cut a length of card, or several thicknesses of foil, long enough to fit around the sponge cake, and about 7.5 cm (3 inches) deep. Fit the card snugly around the sponge, forming square corners as you do so, and secure with sticky tape. Alternatively, place the sponge cake in a deep square cake tin, placing it against two sides of the tin, then form a false 'wall' for the other side, with several thicknesses of foil.

Spoon the whipped ganache on top of the layer of chocolate sponge to a depth of about 5 cm (2 inches) and spread evenly, then place the second layer of sponge on top. Refrigerate for at least 1 hour.

To make the icing, put the chocolate into a small saucepan with the water, the brandy and icing sugar. Stir over a gentle heat until the chocolate melts and blends with the icing sugar to make a smooth icing. Spread the chocolate icing over the top layer of sponge cake and allow to set.

Carefully remove the 'wall' from around the sponge cake. Cut the gâteau into twenty-four 4 cm (1½ inch) squares, using a sharp knife dipped in hot water and dried each time before cutting. Keep chilled until 20–30 minutes before serving.

ORANGES COOKED IN CARAMEL (page 38)

Croquembouche

A spectacular gâteau, served as a wedding cake in France, veiled in a cobweb of fine spun sugar. As the name implies, the gâteau has a crunchy texture from the caramel used to build tiny choux buns into a high pyramid shape. It is best to make a croquembouche in a cool, dry atmosphere, and it should not be completed any longer than 1 hour ahead of serving. However, the choux buns, pastry base, and crème pâtissière can all be made in advance ready for last minute assembly.

double quantity of choux pastry (see page 91)
1 quantity of pâte sucrée (see page 92)
2½ quantities of crème pâtissière (see page 93), flavoured with 45 ml (3 tbsp) Kirsch, or Grand Marnier

450 g (1 lb) granulated sugar
150 ml (¼ pint) water

SERVES TWENTY TO TWENTY-FIVE

Line 3–4 baking sheets with non-stick baking paper.

Put the choux pastry into a large piping bag fitted with a 1 cm (½ inch) plain nozzle. Pipe about 90 small rounds of choux pastry on to the lined baking sheets, each one about 3 cm (1¼ inches) in diameter, and spacing well apart.

Bake in batches (putting those not being baked into the refrigerator while waiting) at 220°C (425°F) mark 7 for 20–25 minutes until well risen, golden brown and crisp. Remove from the oven and pierce each one underneath to allow the steam to escape, then return to the oven for about 5 minutes to dry out. Cool on wire racks. Leave the oven on.

Roll out the pâte sucrée on a lightly floured surface to about 0.5 cm (¼ inch) thick. Place on a baking sheet and prick well all over with a fork. Using a 20.5 cm (8 inch) fluted flan tin, press the sharp edge of the tin into the pastry to cut it into a neat round, then remove the trimmings. Chill for 30 minutes, then bake for 20–25 minutes until very lightly browned. Allow to cool.

Fill a large piping bag, fitted with a 0.5 cm (¼ inch) nozzle, with crème pâtissière. Fill each choux bun with cream, piping it in through the hole made in the bottom. Keep the buns neatly together. Place the pastry round on a flat cake stand.

Put the sugar and water in a heavy-based saucepan and heat gently until the sugar has dissolved, brushing down the sides of the saucepan with hot water. Bring to the boil and boil until it turns a pale caramel colour. Immediately, plunge the base of the saucepan into cold water to stop the caramel cooking further. Then, place the saucepan in a bowl and pour boiling water into the bowl to come about halfway up the side of the saucepan – this will keep the caramel fluid.

Take one of the choux buns and dip one side only in the caramel, then place it, on its side, on the edge of the pastry round, with the filling hole to the centre. Continue until the pastry round is covered. Continue to build up layers of choux buns, making each layer slightly smaller, until all of the buns are used up and you have a high pyramid shape. If necessary, the caramel may be reheated during this process, but do not allow it to darken.

To form the veil, cover a large area of floor with newspaper, then cover the newspaper with sheets of greaseproof paper. Stand the cake stand in the centre of the paper.

If necessary, reheat the remaining caramel until it is liquid again. Holding two or three forks firmly together, dip the forks into the caramel, then lift them out and hold high until the caramel starts to form a very thin thread, then quickly wind the thread around the choux pyramid with a quick, twisting movement – almost throwing it around.

Repeat until all of the caramel has been used up and the choux pyramid is completely covered with a veil of spun sugar. Trim the caramel from around the base of the cake stand with lightly oiled kitchen scissors. Any spun sugar that has gathered in piles on the greaseproof paper should be carefully lifted up and placed on top of the croquembouche. Serve as soon as is possible.

Fresh Fruit Desserts

OF ALL the ingredients available for making desserts, there are none more colourful, or more versatile than fresh fruits. They can easily be transformed into tantalising desserts that few could resist.

Gone are the days when wonderful, exotic fresh fruit desserts were for the summer months only, they can now be part of our winter menus, too. Never before have we been so spoilt for choice. Modern methods of transportation make it possible to enjoy more and more varieties of exotic fruits from all over the world so that fruits like mangoes, pawpaws and passion fruit are now commonplace among the apples and pears.

Although we refer to fruit as being 'in or out of season', this only applies to our own growing seasons. Strawberries are usually ready during June and July, but at other times of the year they are imported from countries such as Israel, Cyprus, Italy, Spain, USA, Kenya and New Zealand, making it possible to buy them practically all year round. The same applies to other fruits.

However, there are still some that only appear for a short while, and there will always be gaps as the seasons change from one country to another, so before deciding on a fresh fruit dessert for a menu, check to see what is available.

You can never guarantee to be able to buy perfectly ripe fruit just when you want it, especially pears, peaches, apricots and mangoes. Buy these a few days beforehand to ensure that they will be ripe when you want to use them. Buy highly perishable fruits, such as raspberries, on the day you need them.

Firmer fruits may be lightly poached in a sugar syrup to soften them, and to bring out their hidden flavours. Most can be made into a purée, perfect for serving as a sauce, or for blending with custard and cream to make ice cream, fools or sorbets. Fruits can be mixed and matched to make an endless variety of fresh fruit salads, sparkling jellies, or even be left to linger on through into the winter months in a deep pot of rum known as a German rumtopf.

Compotes

Compotes are mixtures of fruits cooked in sugar syrup, which can be served hot or cold. The syrup may be flavoured with spices or with orange and lemon rind, but the fruits, being quite highly flavoured themselves, require little or no extra flavouring. Hot compotes make perfect desserts for the winter, not only because they are warming, but also because they are full of vitamins. Chilled compotes will keep well for up to a week in the refrigerator, and may also be used to make a refreshing start to the day by being served with breakfast.

Compotes can be made with a single fruit, but it is more interesting to have a mixture. So that the cooked fruits retain their shape as much as is possible they should be added to the sugar syrup in the order of cooking time – those that need the longest time first, and so on. Always select ripe, but firm fruits. A little liqueur may be added to a compote, just enough to enhance the flavour, not to overpower it.

Basic sugar syrup
**225 g (8 oz) granulated
sugar**

Put the sugar into a saucepan with 300 ml (½ pint) of cold water. Heat very gently until the sugar has completely dissolved, then bring to the boil and boil the syrup for 1 minute.

Spring Compote

Spring rhubarb needs careful cooking. It is very delicate and can easily break up.

basic sugar syrup
40 g (1½ oz) fresh ginger, peeled and finely shredded

1.4 kg (3 lb) rhubarb, cut into 5 cm (2 inch) pieces

SERVES SIX

Make the sugar syrup in a shallow, wide saucepan. Add the ginger and cook gently for 2–3 minutes.

Add just enough rhubarb to make a single layer. Cook gently for 5–6 minutes until just tender, turning the pieces frequently. Transfer to a serving dish. Continue until all the rhubarb is cooked. Boil the syrup until reduced and slightly thickened, then pour it over the rhubarb. Serve the compote hot or cold.

Summer Compote

Serve this compote, well chilled, on bright, hot, sunny days with crème Chantilly. Or, cheer up a gloomy rainy day by serving it hot.

basic sugar syrup
450 g (1 lb) ripe peaches or nectarines, halved, stoned, skinned and cut into thick slices

450 g (1 lb) ripe apricots, skinned, halved and stoned
450 g (1 lb) dark cherries, stoned

SERVES SIX TO EIGHT

Make the sugar syrup in a large wide saucepan. Add the peach slices and cook gently for 10–15 minutes until barely tender. Add the apricots and cook for a further 5 minutes until the apricots just begin to soften. Add the cherries and cook just long enough to soften them without them losing their colour, about 3 minutes.

Carefully transfer the fruits and their syrup to a serving bowl. Cool, then chill.

Autumn Compote

Select very small pears for this compote. Lemon juice added to the syrup prevents the pears and apples discolouring, and adds a tangy flavour.

basic sugar syrup	450 g (1 lb) Victoria
strained juice of 1 lemon	plums, skinned and
450 g (1 lb) small ripe,	stoned
but firm pears	
450 g (1 lb) dessert	SERVES SIX TO EIGHT
apples, Cox or Russet	

Make the sugar syrup in a large saucepan, adding the lemon juice. Thinly peel the pears, cut into half and remove the centre core (if only large pears are available, cut the pears into quarters). Add the pears to the syrup and cook very gently for about 10–15 minutes until barely tender. While the pears are cooking, prepare the apples.

Core the apples with an apple corer, then peel the apples thinly. Cut the apples into halves, then cut into slices across the halves, about 0.5 cm (¼ inch) thick. Add the apple slices to the pears and continue to cook for about 5 minutes until the apple slices are just tender. Add the plums and cook for a further

5 minutes. Carefully transfer the fruits and juice to a serving bowl, taking care not to break up the fruits. Serve the compote hot or cold.

Winter Compote

A compote with a bitter sweet flavour, tangy and refreshing.

basic sugar syrup	175 g (6 oz) black grapes
450 g (1 lb) kumquats,	175 g (6 oz) green grapes
thickly sliced	175 g (6 oz) cranberries
450 g (1 lb) clementines,	
peeled and segmented	SERVES SIX TO EIGHT

Make the sugar syrup in a wide saucepan. Add the kumquats, cover and cook gently for about 15–20 minutes until barely tender.

Add the clementines and grapes, then cook for a further 5 minutes, gently turning the fruits in the syrup and taking care not to break them up. Add the cranberries and cook for about 5 minutes until softened.

Carefully transfer the fruits and syrup to a serving bowl. Serve hot or cold.

Raspberry Sorbet

Loganberries or blackberries may be used instead of raspberries, to make equally delicious sorbets with a rich colour and sharp flavour.

225 g (8 oz) granulated sugar	strained juice of 1 large lemon
150 ml (¼ pint) water	
450 g (1 lb) fresh raspberries	SERVES SIX TO EIGHT

Put the sugar into a saucepan with the water and heat gently until the sugar has dissolved, brushing the sides of the saucepan down with hot water. Bring to the boil and boil for 1 minute. Remove from the heat and allow to cool.

Press the raspberries through a nylon sieve or purée in a blender or food processor then sieve to remove the seeds.

Blend the raspberry purée, lemon juice and the sugar syrup together. Pour into a shallow container and freeze for about 3½ hours, until softly frozen, removing from the freezer every hour and whisking well. Spoon into chilled glasses and serve.

Note
If using a food processor, allow the sorbet to freeze solid, then remove from the freezer and spoon half of it into the processor. Blend until very smooth and creamy, but still softly frozen, remove from the processor and repeat with the remaining half. Spoon the sorbet into chilled glasses and serve immediately. Or, return the sorbet to a container, cover, and freeze for later use. Remove the sorbet from the freezer for 15–20 minutes before serving.

The sorbet can be frozen in an ice cream maker.

Mango and Passion Fruit Sorbet

Although two complementing flavours are used for this sorbet, the distinctive flavour of each one still comes through.

225 g (8 oz) granulated sugar	8 passion fruit
150 (¼ pint) water	strained juice of 1 lemon
5 ripe mangoes	SERVES SIX TO EIGHT

Put the sugar into a saucepan with the water and heat gently until the sugar has dissolved, brushing the sides of the saucepan down with hot water. Bring to the boil and boil for 1 minute. Remove from the heat and allow to cool.

Scoring through the mango skin, in quarters, pull the skin off, then cut the flesh away from the stone. Any ripe flesh that has been pulled away with the skin should be carefully cut away with a small sharp knife. Purée the flesh in a blender or food processor.

Cut the passion fruits in half, then scoop out the seeds with a small spoon into a nylon sieve placed over a small mixing bowl. Work the seeds in the sieve with a spoon to extract all the juice.

Blend the puréed mangoes, passion fruit juice, lemon juice and sugar syrup together, then pour the mixture into a shallow container. Freeze the mixture for about 3½–4 hours until softly frozen, removing from the freezer every hour and whisking well.

Spoon the sorbet into chilled glasses and serve.

Note
If using a food processor, see *Note* for Raspberry sorbet (left).

Pineapple Sorbet

If the pineapple flesh is carefully removed from the centre of the pineapple, so that the skin is left intact, the sorbet may be served in the empty shell. Freeze the empty pineapple shell and the top, for an attractive frosted appearance when serving the sorbet.

225 g (8 oz) granulated
  sugar
150 ml (¼ pint) water
1 large pineapple, to give
  625 g (1 lb 6 oz) of
  prepared fruit, after the
  skin and core are
  removed

strained juice of 2 large
  lemons
strained juice of 1 large
  orange

SERVES SIX TO EIGHT

Put the sugar into a saucepan with the water and heat gently until the sugar has dissolved, brushing the sides of the saucepan with hot water. Bring to the boil and boil for 1 minute. Remove from the heat and allow to cool.

Cut the pineapple flesh into small pieces, then purée in a blender or food processor. Press the purée through a nylon sieve to remove any stringy pieces from the pineapple.

Blend the purée with the lemon and orange juice, and the sugar syrup. Pour into a shallow container and freeze for about 3½ hours until softly frozen, removing from the freezer every hour and whisking well. Spoon the sorbet into well-chilled glasses, or alternatively pile it into the frozen pineapple case, place the pineapple lid on top of the sorbet and serve immediately.

Note

If using a food processor, allow the sorbet to freeze solid, then remove from the freezer and spoon half of it into the processor. Blend until very smooth and creamy, but still softly frozen, remove from the processor and repeat with the remaining half. Spoon the sorbet into chilled glasses and serve immediately. Or, return the sorbet to a container, cover, and freeze for later use. Remove the frozen sorbet from the freezer for 15–20 minutes before serving to allow it to soften a little.

The sorbet can also be frozen in an ice cream maker, if wished.

German Rumtopf

A Rumtopf is a ceramic pot made especially for preserving fresh summer fruits in rum. Rumtopfs came into being as a result of German seafarers trying to take exotic fruits from the West Indies to Germany about 200 years ago.

Each time they tried, the fruits perished during the long voyage. But one day, they found that some fruits at the bottom of a rum barrel, which had either fallen in by chance, or were put there for the purpose of getting the last drop of rum out of the barrel, were perfectly preserved and tasted as if freshly picked from the tree – they had a delicious flavour too! From then on, exotic fruits were transported, in barrels, covered in rum. It wasn't long before German housewives soon learned that they could preserve home-grown fruits in the same way.

Start to make a rumtopf when the first fruits of summer appear, usually strawberries, and continue through the summer months, until the rumtopf is full. A cast-iron will is needed to resist the temptation to taste for two to three months, but it really is worth waiting. The maturing time coincides perfectly with Christmas for a festive treat.

Most fruit can be put into a rumtopf but those with a high water content, such as melon and apple, should be avoided as they can cause fermentation. Also, avoid blackberries, rhubarb and gooseberries, as their sharpness can impart a bitter flavour. All fruits used must be ripe, sound, and very clean.

To begin
450 g (1 lb) caster sugar to every 450 g (1 lb) ripe strawberries, hulled

Thereafter
225 g (8 oz) caster sugar to every 450 g (1 lb) of fruit, such as:-
raspberries, hulled
loganberries, hulled
redcurrants, and blackcurrants, strigged
peaches, skinned halved and stoned
nectarines, skinned, halved and stoned
apricots, skinned, halved and stoned
plums, skinned, halved and stoned
greengages, skinned, halved and stoned
black and green grapes
cherries, stoned
pineapple, skinned, core removed and cut into small pieces
mango, skinned, and cut into dice, or slices
pawpaw, skinned, seeds removed and cut into small slices
kiwi fruits, skinned and sliced
pears, peeled, cored and sliced

1 bottle of rum, no less than 40% alcoholic volume

Wash and thoroughly dry the rumtopf.

Put the strawberries into a large bowl, sprinkle with the caster sugar and mix lightly together. Cover and leave to stand for 1 hour. Put the strawberries, sugar and any juices into the rumtopf and cover with rum to a depth of 1 cm (½ inch).

Cover the surface with clingfilm, then place a saucer on top of the clingfilm to keep the fruit submerged. Cover with more clingfilm, and the rumtopf lid. Put the rumtopf in a cool, airy cupboard.

Continue to add fruits to the rumtopf, soaking them with the stated amount of sugar and rum. When full, cover the rumtopf and store in a cool place for 2–3 months to mature.

SUMMER PUDDING (page 38)

Oranges Cooked in Caramel

Although they are an old favourite, oranges cooked in caramel are still a very popular dessert. Serve with crème Chantilly. If only small oranges are available, allow two per person.

225 g (8 oz) granulated sugar	30–45 ml (2–3 tbsp) Grand Marnier
50 ml (2 fl oz) cold water	crème Chantilly (see page 94), to serve
300 ml (½ pint) boiling water	
6 large oranges	SERVES SIX

Put the sugar into a saucepan with the cold water and heat gently until the sugar has dissolved, brushing down the sides of the saucepan with hot water. Bring to the boil, then boil until the syrup turns a golden caramel colour.

Immediately, plunge the base of the saucepan into cold water to prevent the caramel darkening further. Carefully, pour the boiling water into the pan. Return the caramel to the heat, and heat gently until it has completely dissolved into the water.

Meanwhile, thinly pare the rind from two of the oranges, taking care not to remove the white pith. Cut the rind into very fine shreds and set aside. Using a very sharp knife, remove the skin and white pith from all the oranges.

Put the oranges and the shredded rinds into the caramel, cover and cook them very gently for 25–30 minutes until the oranges are tender, but do not allow to overcook – they must retain a good shape. Turn the oranges frequently during cooking.

Transfer the oranges and their syrup to a large serving dish. Add the Grand Marnier, and allow to cool. Cover and chill.

Summer Pudding

You don't have to wait until summer to enjoy summer pudding; it can be made very successfully with frozen fruits. Traditionally, it is made with bread, but trifle sponge cakes can be used instead. Always make the day before you wish to serve it.

175 g (6 oz) redcurrants, strigged	225 g (8 oz) loganberries, hulled
350 g (12 oz) blackcurrants, strigged	12 thick slices of white bread, about 2 days old, crusts removed
275 g (10 oz) granulated sugar	crème Chantilly (see page 94) to serve
thinly pared rind of 1 large orange, in one continuous spiral if possible	
225 g (8 oz) raspberries, hulled	SERVES EIGHT

Put the red and black currants into a large saucepan with the sugar and orange rind. Cover and cook gently until the juices flow and the sugar has dissolved. Add the raspberries and loganberries, and continue cooking for about 5 minutes until they are softened. Remove from the heat and allow to cool.

Cut a round from one of the slices of bread, large enough to fit in the bottom of a 1.7 litre (3 pint) pudding basin. Place the round in the bottom of the basin, then line the sides of the basin with slightly overlapping slices of bread, reserve the rest for the centre and the top.

Remove the orange rind from the fruit. Spoon half of the fruit and juice into the lined basin, then place a layer of bread on top. Add the remaining fruit and juice, them cover completely with the remaining bread. Cover the bread with clingfilm, then place a small, flat plate on the top. Stand the basin on a plate, to catch any juices that overflow. Place some heavy weights on top of the plate, then chill the pudding overnight.

To serve, gently loosen the pudding from the sides of the basin with a palette knife, then turn out on to a flat plate. Serve with crème Chantilly.

Pears Cooked in Red Wine

Once cooked, the pears will keep very well in a refrigerator for up to a week – improving in flavour as the wine penetrates deeper into them. Always make at least one day before serving.

70 cl bottle of red wine	6 allspice
175 g (6 oz) granulated sugar	6–8 large ripe, but firm, pears
strained juice of 1 large orange	lightly whipped cream, to serve
strained juice of 1 large lemon	
10 cm (4 inch) piece of cinnamon stick	SERVES SIX TO EIGHT

Put the red wine into a large stainless steel saucepan with the sugar, orange and lemon juice, and the spices. Heat gently until the sugar has dissolved, then bring to the boil and boil for 1 minute.

Carefully peel the pears, leaving their stalks on. Put the pears into the spiced wine. Cover and cook gently until the pears are just tender when pierced with the tip of a knife. Turn the pears frequently during cooking.

Using a slotted spoon, transfer the pears to a serving bowl and set aside. Bring the wine to the boil, then boil gently until it is reduced by about half. Pour the reduced wine over the pears, allow to cool, then cover and chill. Serve with lightly whipped cream.

The Perfect Fresh Fruit Salad

Fruit salad can be made with a single fruit, or with a mixture of an indefinite number, according to availability, a combination of three or four fruits that particularly complement each other, or as a tropical mix. Use as many fruits as are available, so that the flavours can intermingle to make a highly perfumed salad, as in this recipe. Do not use bananas in a fruit salad; their very strong flavour will dominate and spoil the overall taste.

450 g (1 lb) granulated sugar
thinly pared rind and strained juice of 1 lemon
600 ml (1 pint) water
2 large dessert apples
3 large pears, peeled
1 small pineapple, skin and core removed, cut into small slices
1 small ripe melon, seeds removed, flesh removed with a melon baller
3 large oranges, skin and all white pith removed, then cut into segments
100 g (4 oz) black grapes, halved and pips removed
100 g (4 oz) green grapes, halved and pips removed

225 g (8 oz) dark sweet cherries, stoned
225 g (8 oz) dessert plums, skinned, stoned and sliced
1 large ripe mango, peeled and cut into thin slices
3 large peaches, skinned, stoned and sliced thinly
225 g (8 oz) strawberries, hulled and sliced
225 g (8 oz) raspberries, hulled
3 kiwi fruit, peeled and sliced
lightly whipped cream, to serve

SERVES TWELVE

Put the sugar and lemon rind in a large saucepan with the water. Heat gently until the sugar has dissolved, then bring to the boil and boil for 5 minutes. Stir in the lemon juice and allow to cool.

Remove the rind, then pour into a bowl.

Quarter, core and thinly slice the apples and pears. Add them to the syrup, then stir in the other fruits. Mix the salad gently, then cover the surface with clingfilm and chill. Serve with cream.

Melon and Figs in Brandy

This simple dessert with its contrasting textures and tastes, is perfect for a hot summer day.

100 g (4 oz) caster sugar
30 ml (2 tbsp) lemon juice
45 ml (3 tbsp) brandy
half a large ripe honeydew melon

12 ripe figs
whipped cream, to serve

SERVES SIX

Put the sugar into a serving bowl with the lemon juice and brandy. Stir until sugar has dissolved.

Remove the seeds from the melon and scoop out the flesh with a melon baller, into the bowl.

Wipe the figs with absorbent kitchen paper. Taste a little piece from one of the figs. If the skin tastes bitter, peel the figs; if the skin does not taste bitter, do not peel. Cut the figs into quarters, then add them to the melon and mix lightly together.

Cover the bowl and leave to stand in a cool place, not the refrigerator, for 2 hours. Serve with cream.

FRESH FRUIT TARTLETS (page 48)

Strawberry and Loganberry Jelly

The subtle taste of puréed strawberries and loganberries combine to make this flavourful jelly. Other fruits can be used in the same way.

225 g (8 oz) granulated
  sugar
300 ml (½ pint) water,
  plus 90 ml (6 tbsp)
450 g (1 lb) strawberries
450 g (1 lb) loganberries
  or raspberries
30 ml (2 tbsp) powdered
  gelatine

Decoration
225 ml (8 fl oz) double
  cream, whipped
fresh strawberries

SERVES EIGHT

Put the sugar into a saucepan with the 300 ml (½ pint) water and heat gently until the sugar has dissolved. Bring to the boil, and boil for 1 minute. Remove from the heat and allow to cool.

Purée the fruits in a blender or food processor, then sieve to remove the seeds.

Sprinkle the gelatine over the remaining water in a small bowl and leave to soften for 2 minutes. Stand in a pan of hot water and stir until dissolved.

Stir the hot gelatine into the sugar syrup, then stir into the fruit purée, until well blended. Pour the jelly mixture into a 1.4 litre (2½ pint) mould and chill until set.

To unmould, dip the mould up to the rim in hot water for 5 seconds, then place a plate upside down over the mould. Invert the two, giving them a good shake. Lift off the mould.

Decorate the jelly with whipped cream and fresh strawberries. Chill until ready to serve.

Blueberry Fool

When blueberries are not available, make this fool with blackcurrants, redcurrants, gooseberries or rhubarb. Rhubarb and gooseberries may be cooked with brown sugar for added flavour. Shortbread fans make a perfect accompaniment.

225 g (8 oz) blueberries or
  blackcurrants
75 g (3 oz) granulated
  sugar
6 egg yolks
25 g (1 oz) caster sugar

300 ml (½ pint) milk
450 ml (¾ pint) double
  cream

SERVES SIX

Put the blueberries and sugar into a saucepan, cover and cook gently until the berries soften. Press through a nylon sieve to purée. Chill.

Lightly whisk the egg yolks and the caster sugar together. Heat the milk until it is almost boiling, then whisk into the egg yolks. Cook the custard over a pan of hot water water until it thickens enough to coat the back of a wooden spoon (or, cook the custard in a microwave oven on full power, for 2½–3 minutes, stirring every 30 seconds with a wire whisk). Immediately the custard thickens, pour it through a nylon sieve into a clean bowl. Cover the surface with clingfilm to prevent a skin forming, cool, then refrigerate until very cold.

Whip the cream until it will hold soft peaks. Mix the chilled purée and custard together until well blended, then carefully fold in the whipped cream. Pour the fool into serving glasses and chill.

Fresh Fruit Purées

When puréed, fruit is transformed into one of its more versatile forms, and can be used as a topping, sauce, flavouring for soufflés, mousses and creams or to make fruit jellies.

Make soft fruits, and cooked fruits, into a purée by simply pressing them through a nylon sieve with the back of a wooden spoon or purée in a blender or food processor. Seeded fruits, such as strawberries, raspberries, and currants, should then be passed through a nylon sieve to remove their seeds. Strawberries have very small seeds, so use the finest mesh sieve you can – or squeeze the purée through muslin.

Firmer fruits, such as peaches, nectarines, apricots, red and black currants, need to be softened first by being cooked with a little water (just sufficient to prevent them sticking) and with a little sugar. Apples, rhubarb, gooseberries, plums and greengages must all be cooked with sugar, until soft, then puréed.

Flambéed Apples Triberg-Style

This wonderful way of cooking apples comes from Triberg, a small picturesque town in the Black Forest – famous for its Kirsch and its clocks! The apples are cooked with honey and lemon, then flambéed with Kirsch, and may be cooked on a spirit burner at the dining table.

6 large dessert apples, Golden Delicious, Cox or Russet
40 g (1½ oz) unsalted butter
25 g (1 oz) caster sugar
thinly pared rind of 1 lemon, taken in one continuous spiral if possible

strained juice of 1 lemon
45 ml (3 tbsp) clear honey
60 ml (4 tbsp) Kirsch
150 ml (¼ pint) double cream, lightly whipped with 15 ml (1 tbsp) Kirsch, to serve

SERVES FOUR TO SIX

Peel, quarter and core the apples. Cut each quarter into half again. Put the butter, sugar, lemon rind and juice and honey into a large shallow saucepan. Heat gently, stirring, until slightly thickened.

Add the apples to the mixture and cook gently, turning the pieces frequently, for 10–15 minutes until the apples are just tender when pierced with the tip of a knife. Spoon the juices into a serving jug and set aside.

Add the Kirsch to the apples, heat for 10 seconds, then set alight. Flambée the apples until the flames begin to subside, then spoon the apples, still slightly flaming, on to hot serving plates. Serve immediately with the juices and whipped cream.

Peaches with Loganberry Sauce

The following method for poaching peach halves can be used for other fruits, such as nectarines, pears, pineapple and plums. The syrup is not needed for the dessert, so store it in a covered container in the refrigerator for poaching other fruits at a later date – eliminating the need to make a fresh syrup. It may be used several times, but should not be used once it becomes discoloured. Fruits should be poached until they are only just tender, as they will continue to cook a little more as they cool in the syrup.

4 very large ripe, but firm
   peaches, halved and
   stoned
350 g (12 oz) granulated
   sugar
600 ml (1 pint) water
1 vanilla bean

Loganberry sauce
225 g (8 oz) loganberries
75 g (3 oz) caster sugar
30 ml (2 tbsp) Kirsch

Topping
175 ml (6 fl oz) double
   cream
2.5 ml (½ tsp) vanilla
   essence
15 ml (1 tbsp) icing sugar
chopped pistachio nuts
   for sprinkling

SERVES FOUR

Put the peach halves into a large bowl and cover with boiling water. Allow to stand for 1 minute, then remove the peaches and peel off their skins.

Put the granulated sugar into a large, wide saucepan with the water and vanilla bean. Heat gently until the sugar has dissolved, then bring to the boil and boil for 2 minutes. Add the peaches and cook very gently, so that the water barely simmers, until the peaches are just tender when pierced with the tip of a knife. Remove from the heat, allow to cool in the syrup. Discard the bean, then chill.

Put the loganberries into a bowl with the caster sugar and Kirsch, mix lightly, then cover and leave to stand for about 1 hour. Press through a nylon sieve to form a purée. Chill.

To serve, whip the cream with the vanilla essence and icing sugar until it will hold soft peaks. Lift the peaches from the syrup with a slotted spoon and allow to drain well. Arrange the peach halves, in pairs, in serving glasses to form an open version of their original shape.

Spoon or pipe the cream into the centre of the peaches, in neat whirls. Pour the loganberry sauce into the bottom of each glass without pouring over the peaches and cream. Sprinkle with nuts and serve immediately.

APRICOT FLAN (page 50)

Tarts and Pies

FROM a humble pie to the most exquisite flan filled with exotic fruits, tarts and pies are popular the world over. But, classifying just what is a tart, and what is a pie, can cause some confusion. Each one has a different image, depending on which country you live in and even within each country itself.

Tart (or flan)

Technically speaking, a tart, or a flan, is an open pastry case filled with fruit, cream or a custard filling. They can be as simple as a round of pastry placed on a baking sheet and topped with fruit. Or, the pastry can be formed in a metal flan ring, or flan tin, to make an attractive container perfect for filling. The pastry used for tarts or flans may be rich shortcrust pastry, pàte sucrée, or almond pastry. The pastry case may be filled before baking, but more often that not, it is baked 'blind' (without a filling) to be filled when it is cooked.

It may be baked blind with, or without, baking beans to weight the pastry down and keep it in shape. If the pastry is well formed, and chilled before baking it shouldn't be necessary to use baking beans, but to simply prick the pastry well over the base and up the sides with a fork. However, if using beans remove them for the last 5–10 minutes baking, for the pastry to dry completely. When a pastry case is to be filled with a custard mixture, it is advisable to partially bake it blind before adding the filling.

Pies

A pie is defined as having a bottom, sides and top, containing a filling. It can be made with a single pastry crust, to cover fruit in a deep pie dish or, be made with a double crust – pastry top and bottom – in a shallow dish.

Pies can be round, oval, oblong, or square. Sweet pies are usually made with either shortcrust pastry, or rich shortcrust pastry. Double crust pies may have a cleverly interwoven top, made with strips of pastry. A solid top may be left plain, or be decorated with pastry leaves, or other pretty shapes.

Pie edges always look better when decorated. The edge can be tapped lightly with a small knife to give a flaked effect, known as 'knocking up' the edge. It can be shaped into scallops by pulling it in at intervals with the tip of a knife.

A pie with a sweet filling should have the scallops made fairly small, and close together – as opposed to a pie with a savoury filling where the scallops are larger and wider apart (a tradition handed down from years gone by, when it was a means of identifying whether a pie had a sweet filling or a savoury filling; probably in the old pie-making shops). A simple decorative edge can be made by pinching the 'knocked up' edge between your forefinger and thumb, or with a pair of pastry crimpers.

The pastry may be glazed with beaten egg or milk before baking, or left unglazed and then sprinkled with caster sugar immediately the pie is removed from the oven. A small hole should always be made in the top of a pie to allow the steam inside to escape.

Fillings

It would be an almost impossible task to list all of the fillings suitable for tarts and pies. The varieties are endless, but they do fall into three categories – fruit, cream and custards.

Double crust pies and lattice-topped pies can be filled with uncooked or pre-cooked fruits.

Uncooked fruit benefits from being tossed in a little flour, as the flour will thicken the juice from the fruit as the pie cooks. Ground almonds sprinkled over the bottom layer of pastry for a fruit pie will help to prevent the pastry from becoming soggy.

Flan cases are particularly good for filling with fresh fruits, any type of cream or mousse mixture. Flavoured and spiced custard mixtures can be baked in a pastry case until set.

The French are particularly famous for their flans, especially those filled with fresh fruits. Their most famous flan must be the apple flan from Normandy (see page 50) as well as many others that contain a sweetened custard and fruit.

The English have long prided themselves on their apple pies. We boast of having the best flavoured apples, so our pies should be good! The Elizabethans added wine to their apple pies, and there's no reason why we shouldn't too. The next time you cook apples prior to putting them into a pie, add a little red or white wine. It has also long been the custom to add spices and flavourings, such as lemon and orange rind.

Fresh Fruit Tartlets

These colourful little tartlets can be made with any fresh fruits you like. Raspberries can be sifted with icing sugar instead of being glazed.

1 quantity of almond pastry (see page 92)	**Apricot glaze**
half quantity of crème pâtissière (see page 93)	225 g (8 oz) apricot conserve
100 g (4 oz) dark, well-flavoured, cherries, stoned and halved	15 ml (1 tbsp) Kirsch
	Redcurrant glaze
100 g (4 oz) black grapes, halved and deseeded	100 g (4 oz) redcurrant jelly
100 g (4 oz) green grapes, halved and deseeded	MAKES TWELVE
2 kiwi fruit, peeled and sliced	

Roll out the pastry on a lightly floured surface and cut out twelve 12.5 cm (5 inch) circles with a round cutter and use to line twelve 10 cm (4 inch) tartlet tins. Trim the edges and prick the base of each tartlet with a fork, then place the lined tins on baking sheets and chill for at least 30 minutes.

Bake blind at 220°C (425°F) mark 7 for 20–25 minutes until very lightly browned. Allow the cases to cool a little in their tins, then carefully transfer to a wire rack to cool.

Make the apricot glaze (see page 94), then brush it evenly over the inside of each pastry case. Reserve the remaining glaze.

Divide the crème pâtissière equally between the pastry cases and spread it evenly. Arrange the cherries attractively in three of the cases, the grapes in six, and the kiwi fruit in the remaining ones.

Reheat the remaining apricot glaze until boiling, then carefully brush it over the green grapes and the kiwi fruit to glaze them evenly. Heat the redcurrant jelly until boiling, then carefully brush it over the cherries and the black grapes.

Once glazed, the fruits may be sprinkled with finely chopped nuts or a few toasted flaked almonds, if liked. Serve as soon as possible.

FRENCH APPLE FLAN (Page 50)

Apricot Flan

It is best to use fresh apricots for this flan, but you can use canned or bottled ones.

---

about 17 fresh apricots, poached or use 34 canned or bottled apricot halves	10 ml (2 tsp) caster sugar
	15 ml (1 tbsp) apricot jam
30 ml (2 tbsp) Kirsch	*Decoration*
1 quantity of pâte sucrée (see page 92)	150 ml (¼ pint) double cream
100 ml (4 fl oz) single cream	25 g (1 oz) plain chocolate, melted
1 egg	SERVES SIX TO EIGHT

Put the apricot halves into a bowl, sprinkle with the Kirsch, cover and leave to stand for about 1 hour.

Roll out the pâte sucrée on a lightly floured surface to a round, 2.5 cm (1 inch) larger than a 23 cm (9 inch) fluted flan tin. Line the tin with the pastry, pressing it well into the flutes. Trim the edge, and prick the pastry all over with a fork. Chill for 30 minutes, then partially bake at 220°C (425°F) mark 7 for 20 minutes.

Meanwhile, drain the apricots, reserving any Kirsch. Lightly whisk the cream with the egg, caster sugar and remaining Kirsch.

Remove the partially baked flan case from the oven. Reduce the oven temperature to 190°C (375°F) mark 5. Leaving the pastry case in the flan tin, spread the apricot jam over the bottom of the flan. Reserve six apricot halves for decoration, then arrange the rest on top of the jam. Pour in the custard mixture. Bake for 30–40 minutes until the custard is set. Cool.

Whip the double cream for the decoration until it will hold soft peaks. Transfer the flan to a serving plate and spread the cream evenly over the top. Put the melted chocolate into a small paper piping bag, then cut a small hole in the bottom of the bag. Pipe the chocolate, in criss-cross lines, across the cream. Cut each of the reserved apricot halves in half and arrange neatly around the edge of the flan on the cream to decorate.

French Apple Flan

Because it is attributed to the apple growing region of France, this flan is sometimes called Normandy Apple Flan. This recipe, which is just one of many versions, uses two types of apples, cooked in different ways, each one contrasting with the other. If you do not have Calvados (an apple brandy) use brandy.

---

900 g (2 lb) cooking apples	4–5 large Golden Delicious, Russet or Cox apples
175 g (6 oz) granulated sugar	50 g (2 oz) caster sugar
30 ml (2 tbsp) water	half quantity apricot glaze (see page 94)
50 g (2 oz) stoned raisins	crème Chantilly (see page 94), to serve
60 ml (4 tbsp) Calvados	
1 quantity pâte sucrée (see page 92)	SERVES EIGHT

Peel, quarter, core and slice the cooking apples and put into a large saucepan with the granulated sugar and water. Cover and cook gently for about 20 minutes until the apples become soft and fluffy. Pour the cooked apples into a nylon sieve placed over a bowl; allow to drain and cool. (The apple juice will not be needed.)

Put the raisins into a small saucepan with the Calvados and cook gently for 2–3 minutes to soften the raisins. Allow to cool.

Roll out the pâte sucrée on a lightly floured surface to a round, 2.5 cm (1 inch) larger than a 25 cm (10 inch) fluted flan tin. Line the tin with the pastry, pressing it well into the flutes. Trim the edges.

Beat the cooked apples until fairly smooth, then fold in the raisins and Calvados. Spread the apple mixture evenly over the bottom of the pastry case. Peel and core the Golden Delicious apples. Cut each apple in half, then cut each half into thin slices.

Arrange the apple slices in concentric circles on top of the cooked apple mixture. Sprinkle the apple slices with caster sugar. Bake at 220°C (425°F) mark 7 for 30–35 minutes until the pastry is cooked, and the apple slices are tender and very lightly browned.

Heat the apricot glaze until boiling. Immediately the flan is removed from the oven, brush the apricot glaze evenly over the apple slices. Allow the flan to cool to room temperature before serving. Serve with lightly whipped crème Chantilly.

Strawberry Flan

This classic, French strawberry flan is simplicity itself, but you must use full-flavoured strawberries and a good strawberry conserve to produce the best results.

1 quantity of almond pastry (see page 92)	lightly whipped cream, to serve
500 g (1 lb 2 oz) strawberry conserve	SERVES EIGHT
45 ml (3 tbsp) Cointreau	
700 g (1½ lb) medium-sized, fresh strawberries, hulled	

Roll out the almond pastry on a lightly floured surface to a round, 2.5 cm (1 inch) larger than a 25 cm (10 inch) fluted flan tin. Line the tin with the pastry, pressing it well into the flutes. Trim the edges, then prick the pastry all over. Chill for at least 30 minutes, then bake at 220°C (425°F) mark 7 for 25–30 minutes until very lightly browned. Allow to cool.

Put the strawberry conserve into a saucepan, heat gently until melted, then sieve through a nylon sieve into another clean saucepan. Stir in the Cointreau and bring to the boil.

Brush a little of the strawberry glaze over the bottom and up the sides of the flan case. Put the pastry case on a flat serving plate. Arrange the strawberries, pointed ends up, neatly in the flan case. Spoon the remaining strawberry glaze over the strawberries until they are all evenly coated. Serve with lightly whipped cream.

Whisky Mocha Flan

This flan is made with a coffee-flavoured bavarois mixture, topped with whisky cream, and elegantly decorated with chocolate caraque.

half quantity of rich shortcrust pastry (see page 88)	15 ml (1 tbsp) caster sugar
150 g (5 oz) plain chocolate	150 ml (¼ pint) double cream
10 ml (2 tsp) powdered gelatine	*Topping*
30 ml (2 tbsp) water	200 ml (7 fl oz) double cream
150 ml (¼ pint) milk	15–30 ml (1–2 tbsp) whisky
15 ml (1 tbsp) coffee granules	15 ml (1 tbsp) caster sugar
3 egg yolks	SERVES SIX TO EIGHT

Roll out the pastry on a lightly floured surface to a round 2.5 cm (1 inch) larger than a 23 cm (9 inch) fluted flan tin. Line the tin with the pastry, pressing it well into the flutes. Trim the edges then prick the pastry with a fork. Chill for 30 minutes, then bake blind at 220°C (425°F) mark 7 for 20–25 minutes until the pastry is cooked and very lightly browned. Allow to cool.

Break the chocolate into small pieces and put into a small bowl over a pan of hot water until the chocolate melts. Stir until smooth.

Remove the pastry case from the flan tin and place it, upside-down, on a sheet of greaseproof paper. Using a pastry brush, brush some of the melted chocolate evenly all over the pastry case. Leave in a cool place until the chocolate sets. Turn the flan case over and brush the inside with more chocolate and allow to set.

Spread out the remaining chocolate thinly on a marble slab, or on thick waxed paper and leave to set until it no longer sticks to your hand when you touch it. Holding a large knife with both hands, push the blade across the surface of the chocolate to roll pieces off in long curls. Adjust the angle of the blade to get the best curls. Put the curls on a plate and chill until needed.

Sprinkle the gelatine over the water in a small bowl and leave to soften.

Put the milk and the coffee granules into a small saucepan, heat gently until the coffee dissolves completely, and the milk comes almost to the boil. Very lightly whisk the egg yolks and the caster sugar together in a bowl, then stir in the coffee-flavoured milk until well combined.

Place the bowl over a pan of hot water and cook the custard, stirring continuously, until thick enough to coat the back of the spoon, (alternatively, cook the custard in a microwave oven on full power for 2–2½ minutes, stirring every 30 seconds).

Immediately the custard thickens, strain it through a nylon sieve into a clean bowl. Add the soaked gelatine and stir until dissolved. Allow the custard to cool, stirring frequently to prevent a skin forming.

Whip the cream until it will just hold soft peaks, then gently fold it into the coffee custard. Place the chocolate coated flan case on a flat serving plate, fill with the coffee cream mixture, then chill until set.

Make the topping, whip the cream with the whisky and sugar until it will just hold soft peaks, then spread an even layer of cream over the top of the flan. Whip the remaining cream until thick enough to pipe and fill a piping bag fitted with a medium sized star nozzle. Pipe whirls of cream around the top of the flan, then decorate with the chocolate caraque. Chill until ready to serve.

WHISKY MOCHA FLAN (above)

Tray-Bake Tarts

These tarts, are reminiscent of the ones made in a little café in Switzerland. In the autumn, they make huge trays of plum tarts and serve portions topped with a mound of whipped cream nearly as big as the Jungfrau mountain that one sits and admires from the café terrace. Once you have made one tart, you will soon realize that you do not really need a recipe to follow. You simply roll out rich shortcrust pastry as large, or as small as you wish, to fit your baking sheet. The pastry is then covered with apples, plums, halved pears or apricots, sprinkled with sugar and baked – easy to make, and so delicious to eat! Use marmalade for apple tart or apricot glaze (see page 94) for the other fruit.

1 quantity of rich shortcrust pastry (see page 88)	100 g (4 oz) caster sugar
700–900 g (1½–2 lb) cooking apples	60 ml (4 tbsp) fine shred marmalade
40–50 g (1½–2 oz) ground almonds	lightly whipped cream, to serve
	MAKES EIGHT TO TEN SLICES

Roll out the pastry on a lightly floured surface to an oblong about 30×33 cm (12×13 inches), or if your baking sheet is very flat – roll the pastry out on the baking sheet directly. Place the pastry on the baking sheet, then turn in the edge about 1 cm (½ inch) to form a small edge, pinch the pastry edge with your forefinger and thumb, to decorate.

Core and peel the apples and slice into rings about 0.5 cm (¼ inch) thick. Sprinkle the ground almonds

over the pastry, then arrange the apple rings, overlapping, in neat rows on top. Sprinkle with caster sugar, then bake at 220°C (425°F) mark 7 for 30–35 minutes until the pastry is cooked and lightly browned, and the apples are tender.

Heat the marmalade until boiling, then brush it evenly over the hot apples to glaze. Serve the tart cut into slices, with a generous portion of lightly whipped cream on each one.

Angostura Pie

Normally associated with pink gin and hangovers, Angostura bitters is surprisingly good when it is sweetened and mixed with cream – as it is in this creamy pie.

1 quantity of pâte sucrée (see page 92)	*Decoration*
15 ml (1 tbsp) powdered gelatine	150 ml (¼ pint) crème Chantilly (see page 94)
45 ml (3 tbsp) water	14–16 pistachio nuts, skinned
2 eggs, separated	
50 g (2 oz) caster sugar	
22.5 ml (1½ tbsp) Angostura bitters	SERVES SIX TO EIGHT
300 ml (½ pint) double cream	

Roll out the pâte sucrée on a lightly floured surface and use to line a deep 20.5 cm (8 inch) pie plate or flan dish. Trim and decorate the edge. Prick the pastry all over with a fork. Chill for 30 minutes, then bake blind 220°C (425°F) mark 7 for 20–25 minutes until the pastry is cooked. Allow to cool.

Sprinkle the gelatine over the water in a small bowl and leave to soften for 2 minutes. Meanwhile, whisk the egg yolks with the caster sugar until very thick, then whisk in the Angostura bitters.

Stand the bowl of gelatine in a small saucepan of hot water and stir until dissolved. Whip the cream until it will hold soft peaks. Whisk the egg whites until they are quite foamy, but not too stiff.

Whisk the gelatine into the Angostura mixture, then carefully fold in the cream and the egg whites. Pour the mixture, immediately, into the pie case. Chill until set.

Whip the crème Chantilly until thick enough to pipe, then fill a piping bag fitted with a large star nozzle. Pipe rosettes, or stars, of cream on top of the pie, then decorate with pistachio nuts. Chill the pie until ready to serve.

Old-Fashioned Apple Pie

This is the sort of pie our grandmothers used to make – simple and straightforward, but full of flavour. Serve the pie warm, with a real egg custard. Blackberry, blackberry and apple, and rhubarb pies can be made in exactly the same way.

about 900 g (2 lb) cooking apples	8–12 cloves
150 g (5 oz) granulated sugar	1 quantity of shortcrust pastry (see page 88)
25 g (1 oz) plain flour	caster sugar for sprinkling
finely grated rind of 1 lemon	
30 ml (2 tbsp) lemon juice	SERVES FOUR

Peel, quarter and slice the apples and put into a large bowl with the granulated sugar, flour, lemon rind, lemon juice and cloves. Toss gently together.

Roll out the pastry on a lightly floured surface to an oval, about 5 cm (2 inches) larger than the top of a 1.1 litre (2 pint) pie dish. Cut a 2.5 cm (1 inch) strip from the outer edge and place it on the dampened rim of the dish.

Fill the pie dish with the apple mixture, forming it into a neat mound. Brush the pastry strip with water, then carefully cover the pie dish with the remaining pastry, pressing the pastry edges together well to seal. Trim the pastry from around the edge of the pie with a small sharp knife, holding the knife at an angle pointed away from the pie.

Pressing firmly around the edge of the pastry, gently tap the pastry with a small knife to flake the edge, then decorate the edge by pulling it into small scallops with the tip of the knife. Make a small hole in the centre of the pie to allow the steam to escape. Chill for about 30 minutes.

Bake at 220°C (425°F) mark 7 for 10 minutes, then reduce the oven temperature to 200°C (400°F) mark 6 and continue cooking for 30–35 minutes until the pastry is golden brown, and the apples are cooked.

Immediately the pie is removed from the oven, sift caster sugar evenly over the top.

Hot Soufflés

AS WITH time, a hot soufflé waits for no man – even the most exalted in the land must wait for a soufflé.

To some, a hot soufflé means a dramatic end to a dinner, as is certainly the case when a golden, puffed-up masterpiece is triumphantly carried to the dining table. Others prefer to serve a hot soufflé at a cosy, more intimate dinner for two or four, especially during the winter, when it makes the perfect dessert – warming, yet very light. Making a soufflé in a more relaxed atmosphere means that there is less risk of embarrassment if it fails to rise to one's expectations. When the cook is not under any stress they always rise well!

A hot soufflé is the true soufflé. In a cold soufflé the tiny bubbles of air, trapped within the egg whites, are set in suspension by the gelatine. With a hot soufflé, the tiny air bubbles expand as they are heated, puffing up the base mixture, to which they were added, by as much as two-thirds of its original size.

The base for a sweet soufflé is usually a flavoured sauce, enriched with egg yolks, anything from a subtle vanilla, through a whole range of fruit purées, to the stronger flavours of coffee and chocolate. The sauce must be just the right consistency for incorporating egg whites – neither thick, nor thin. Having said that, soufflés can be more simply made with fruit purée and meringue, though using a slightly different technique (see the next page).

The success of a soufflé depends on the egg whites being whisked to the right degree, and how they are added to the base mixture. They should be whisked until they are stiff enough to hold a stiff, unwavering, peak on the end of a whisk, yet still be very smooth. Egg whites whisked by hand in a copper bowl produce a greater volume, and have a much stronger make up. A proportion of the sugar is whisked into the whites, to make them into a light meringue, which is stronger and smoother.

A little of the whisked whites should always be added to the sauce base to loosen the mixture, and make easier to fold in the remaining whites. If the saucepan is large enough, the whites can all be added to the sauce in the pan. Always fold the egg whites into the base mixture very carefully, and very lightly. The more bubbles you retain within the mixture, the lighter the soufflé will be, and the more it will rise. Fold the whites in with a large metal spoon, or a rubber spatular.

Hot soufflés are normally baked in straight-sided ovenproof dishes. A soufflé dish should be buttered well and then be lightly coated with caster sugar. Only use butter, other fats would spoil the flavour of the soufflé. Buttering the dish enables the soufflé mixture to rise up the side of the dish without sticking, so that it can go on rising above the top of the dish until it reaches its maximum height and sets. The sugar keeps the side of the soufflé moist.

It is not necessary to put a paper collar around a dish for a hot soufflé, providing the mixture is of the right consistency it will support itself. Removing a paper collar puts the soufflé in danger of collapsing more quickly, and of being damaged by pulling a chunk out of the side with the paper. Stand the soufflé dish on a baking sheet, to help to transmit the heat more quickly through the dish, and to make it easier to remove from the oven when it is ready.

A soufflé can be baked until it is just set and still slightly moist in the centre, or until completely set. Do not over bake a soufflé, it will become very dry. Cooking in a moderate oven means that the soufflé cooks evenly throughout. In a hot oven, it would rise quickly, form a crisp outside and have a soft centre. To test for doneness, insert a long thin skewer into the centre of the soufflé – if it comes out moist, the soufflé will be slightly soft, if it comes out clean, the soufflé will be set right through to the centre.

Soufflés are usually sifted with icing sugar as soon as they are taken out of the oven, so always have the sugar and a small sieve nearby. Serve the soufflé on a doily-lined plate, this makes it look more attractive, and also easier to carry to the table. Serving the soufflé with a complementing sauce makes it even more delicious.

Other soufflés

A soufflé made simply with meringue and a fruit purée is mixed in a slightly different way to other soufflés. As it is quite difficult to fold whites into a thin mixture, the purée is gradually mixed into the whites. As the whites are made into a strong meringue, they can withstand the extra mixing.

Steamed soufflés, instead of being baked in the oven, are gently steamed in a fairly deep saucepan in a bain-marie on top of the cooker. The slow moist cooking sets the soufflé firm enough to be turned out, yet still wonderfully light, and with certainly no fear of it collapsing before it reaches the table.

With a soufflé omelette the yolks are whisked with sugar and flavouring until very thick then mixed with a little flour. The whites are whisked in the normal way before being added to the yolks. The mixture is cooked briefly in an omelette pan on top of the stove before being baked in the oven.

Soufflé mixtures can also be used as a filling for small pancakes; or be baked in scooped out orange cases.

Steamed Chocolate Soufflé with Chocolate Sauce

Those who have a passion for chocolate will find that this soufflé, with its rich chocolate sauce, will transport them to 'seventh heaven'!

25 g (1 oz) unsalted butter	30 ml (2 tbsp) brandy
25 g (1 oz) plain flour	150 ml (¼ pint) milk
150 ml (¼ pint) milk	150 ml (¼ pint) double
75 g (3 oz) plain	cream
chocolate, chopped	15 g (½ oz) unsalted
finely	butter
25 g (1 oz) caster sugar	10 ml (2 tsp) cornflour,
75 ml (3 fl oz) double	plus 15 ml (1 tbsp) milk
cream	for mixing
3 egg yolks	
4 egg whites	SERVES SIX
icing sugar for sifting	

Chocolate sauce
75 g (3 oz) plain
   chocolate, chopped
   finely

Grease a 15 cm (6 inch), 7.5 cm (3 inch) deep, soufflé dish with butter, then coat evenly with a little caster sugar.

Melt the butter in a saucepan, then stir in the flour. Gradually stir in the milk, then add the chocolate. Heat gently, stirring all the time, until the chocolate melts, then bring to the boil and boil until thickened. Remove the sauce from the heat, beat in half the sugar, then the cream and the egg yolks.

Whisk the egg whites until stiff, but not dry, then gradually whisk in the remaining sugar, whisking until shiny. Add about one-third of the egg whites to the chocolate mixture and fold in carefully to loosen the mixture, then very gently fold in the remaining egg whites.

Pour the soufflé mixture into the prepared dish. Place a trivet in a heavy-based saucepan, stand the soufflé dish on the trivet, then add enough boiling water to come about one-third of the way up the side of the dish. Cover the pan with a tightly fitting lid, then steam the soufflé gently for 45 minutes, until it is well risen and set.

Meanwhile, make the chocolate sauce, put the chocolate, brandy, milk and cream into a small saucepan. Heat gently, stirring until the chocolate melts, then stir in the butter.

Blend the cornflour with the milk to form a smooth paste, then stir it into the sauce. Cook over a moderate heat until the sauce thickens slightly. Keep the sauce warm until ready to serve – to prevent a skin forming, cover the surface of the sauce closely with clingfilm.

When the soufflé is cooked, turn the heat off under the pan and allow the soufflé to settle for 5 minutes. Turn the soufflé out on to a warmed serving dish. Sift icing sugar over the top. Serve immediately, with the chocolate sauce poured around it, or served separately in a jug.

Apricot Soufflé with Apricot Sauce

Canned or bottled apricot halves can be used for this recipe. Purée the apricots with their juice in a blender or food processor to get the best results.

25 g (1 oz) unsalted butter	*Apricot sauce*
25 g (1 oz) plain flour	225 g (8 fl oz) apricot
225 ml (8 fl oz) apricot	purée
purée	15 ml (1 tbsp) Grand
50 g (2 oz) caster sugar	Marnier
3 egg yolks	15 ml (1 tbsp) caster sugar
4 egg whites	5 ml (1 tsp) arrowroot
icing sugar for sifting	
	SERVES FOUR TO SIX

Grease a 15 cm (6 inch), 5 cm (2½ inch) deep, soufflé dish with butter, then coat evenly with a little caster sugar.

Melt the butter in a saucepan, add the flour, then gradually stir in the apricot purée. Bring the sauce to the boil, stirring, and boil until the mixture thickens. Remove the sauce from the heat and beat in half the caster sugar, then the egg yolks.

Whisk the egg whites until stiff, but not dry, then gradually whisk in the remaining caster sugar, whisking until shiny. Gradually fold the egg whites into the apricot sauce until no trace of white remains.

Pour the soufflé mixture into the prepared dish. Stand the dish on a baking sheet, then bake in the centre of the oven at 180°C (350°F) mark 4 for about 40 minutes, until very well risen, and just lightly set.

Meanwhile, make the apricot sauce, put the apricot purée, Grand Marnier, and sugar into a small saucepan. Blend the arrowroot with a little cold water to make a smooth paste, then stir into the apricot mixture. Bring the sauce to the boil, stirring until the mixture thickens and clears. Pour the sauce into a warmed serving jug and keep hot.

When the soufflé is cooked, remove from the oven and sift icing sugar lightly over the top. Serve immediately with the apricot sauce poured around it, or served separately in a jug.

Vanilla Soufflé

Serve this very light vanilla soufflé with lightly whipped crème Chantilly, a fruit sauce, or a vanilla-flavoured custard.

25 g (1 oz) unsalted butter	3 egg yolks
25 g (1 oz) plain flour	4 egg whites
150 ml (¼ pint) milk	icing sugar for sifting
50 g (2 oz) caster sugar	
30 ml (2 tbsp) double	SERVES 4
cream	
5 ml (1 tsp) vanilla	
essence	

Grease a 15 cm (6 inch), 7.5 cm (3 inch) deep, soufflé dish with butter, then coat evenly with a little caster sugar.

Melt the butter in a saucepan, add the flour, then gradually stir in the milk. Bring the sauce to the boil, stirring until the mixture thickens. Remove from the heat and beat in half the sugar, the double cream, vanilla essence, and then the egg yolks.

Whisk the egg whites until they are stiff, but not dry, then gradually whisk in the remaining caster sugar, whisking until shiny. Fold the egg whites into the vanilla sauce.

Pour the soufflé mixture into the prepared dish, then stand the dish on a baking sheet. Bake in the centre of the oven at 180°C (350°F) mark 4 for 45–50 minutes until the soufflé is very well risen, and lightly set. Remove from the oven and sift icing sugar lightly over the top. Serve immediately.

Orange and Grand Marnier Soufflé

Serve this classic soufflé with very lightly whipped cream flavoured with Grand Marnier.

grated rind of 2 large oranges	3 egg yolks
150 ml (¼ pint) milk	4 egg whites
25 g (1 oz) unsalted butter	icing sugar for sifting
25 g (1 oz) plain flour	
50 g (2 oz) caster sugar	SERVES 4
30 ml (2 tbsp) Grand Marnier	

Put the grated rind into a saucepan with the milk, bring almost to the boil, then remove from the heat, cover and leave to stand for 30 minutes, or longer if possible.

Grease a 15 cm (6 inch), 6 cm (2½ inch) deep, soufflé dish with butter, then coat evenly with a little caster sugar.

Strain the milk through a small nylon sieve to remove the rind. Melt the butter in a saucepan, add the flour, then gradually stir in the orange-flavoured milk. Bring to the boil, stirring until the mixture thickens. Remove the sauce from the heat and beat in half the sugar, the Grand Marnier, and then the egg yolks.

Whisk the egg whites until they are stiff, but not dry, then gradually whisk in the remaining caster sugar, whisking until shiny. Fold the egg whites into the orange sauce.

Pour the soufflé mixture into the prepared dish, then stand the dish on a baking sheet. Bake in the centre of the oven at 180°C (350°F) mark 4 for 35–40 minutes until the soufflé is very well risen and lightly set. Remove from the oven and sift icing sugar lightly over the top. Serve immediately.

OLD ENGLISH SYLLABUB (page 71)

Soufflé Pancakes with Blackberry Sauce

These little pancakes, filled with a tangy lemon mixture and baked, served with a blackberry sauce, are quite delicious. A supply of pancakes and blackberry sauce in the freezer, will make this a speedy dessert to prepare.

50 g (2 oz) plain flour
a pinch of salt
1 egg
150 ml (¼ pint) milk
15 g (½ oz) unsalted
  butter, melted
15 ml (1 tbsp) brandy
butter for frying

Blackberry sauce
225 g (8 oz) fresh or
  frozen blackberries
50–75 g (2–3 oz) caster
  sugar

Soufflé filling
2 egg yolks
50 g (2 oz) caster sugar
finely grated rind of
  1 lemon
15 ml (1 tbsp) strained
  lemon juice
20 g (¾ oz) plain flour,
  sifted
3 egg whites
icing sugar for sifting

SERVES FOUR TO EIGHT

Sift the flour and salt into a mixing bowl and make a well in the centre. Break the egg into the centre, then gradually whisk into the flour, adding the milk as the mixture thickens. When the batter is smooth, mix in the melted butter and brandy. Cover and leave to stand for about 30 minutes.

Heat a little butter in a 15 cm (6 inch) heavy-based frying pan, then pour off any excess. Pour in just enough batter to thinly cover the base of the pan, cook for about 1 minute until the batter is set, and the pancake is lightly browned on the underside, turn or toss the pancake and cook the other side for about 1 minute until lightly browned. Transfer the pancake to a plate and cover with a sheet of absorbent kitchen paper or greaseproof paper. Make seven more pancakes in the same way, placing paper between each one.

To make the sauce, sieve the blackberries through a nylon sieve into a small saucepan, then stir in the caster sugar to taste. Set aside until needed.

To make the soufflé filling, and complete the pancakes, butter a 23×28 cm (9×11 inch) ovenproof dish. Whisk the egg yolks with half the caster sugar and the lemon rind until very thick, then whisk in the lemon juice. Fold in the flour. Whisk the egg whites until stiff, then gradually whisk in the remaining sugar, whisking until shiny. Fold the egg whites into the lemon mixture.

Spread the pancakes out on a work surface and divide the soufflé mixture equally between them, spooning it along the centre of each one. Bring the sides of each pancake up over the filling, until they just overlap. Place the pancakes side-by-side in the buttered dish, sift lightly with icing sugar, then bake in the centre of the oven at 190°C (375°F) mark 5 for 12–15 minutes until the soufflé mixture is well risen and lightly firm to the touch.

Meanwhile, heat the blackberry sauce and pour it into a warmed serving jug. Remove the cooked pancakes from the oven and sift lightly with more icing sugar. Serve immediately, with the hot blackberry sauce.

Raspberry Soufflé

Made simply with puréed raspberries, sugar and egg whites, this soufflé has a lovely fresh fruit flavour. Serve with a little lightly whipped cream, if liked.

225 g (8 oz) fresh raspberries
3 egg whites
75 g (3 oz) caster sugar

icing sugar for sifting

SERVES FOUR

Grease a 15 cm (6 inch), 6 cm (2½ inch) deep, soufflé dish with butter, then coat evenly with a little caster sugar. Sieve the raspberries through a nylon sieve to make a purée, about 225 ml (8 fl oz).

Whisk the egg whites until stiff, but not dry, then gradually whisk in the caster sugar, whisking until shiny. Fold the raspberry purée into the egg whites.

Pour the soufflé mixture into the prepared soufflé dish and mark into a swirl on the top. Stand the dish on a baking sheet, then bake at 180°C (350°F) mark 4 for about 20 minutes, until lightly set. Remove from the oven and sift icing sugar lightly over the top. Serve immediately.

Salzburger Nockerln

This is a speciality of the Salzkammergut region of Austria. The soufflé is baked in a shallow dish, about 2.5 cm (1 inch) deep, and is mounded in the dish to represent the mountains of the area.

3 egg yolks
finely grated rind of 2 lemons
30 ml (2 tbsp) strained lemon juice
25 g (1 oz) plain flour, sifted

4 egg whites
50 g (2 oz) caster sugar
icing sugar for sifting

SERVES 4

Butter a shallow 23 cm (9 inch) round, or oval, dish.

Whisk the egg yolks and lemon rind together until they are thickened, then whisk in the lemon juice and fold in the flour.

Whisk the egg whites until they are stiff, but not dry, then gradually whisk in the caster sugar, whisking until shiny. Fold a little of the egg whites into the lemon mixture to loosen it, then carefully fold in the rest.

Spoon the soufflé mixture, in three mounds, in the prepared dish. Place the dish on a baking sheet and bake in the centre of the oven at 190°C (375°F) mark 5 for 12–14 minutes until lightly set. Remove from the oven and sift icing sugar lightly over the top. Serve immediately.

Creams, Mousses and Cold Soufflés

AWE-INSPIRING soufflés, beautifully moulded bavarois, and rich, light mousses are wonderful creations, guaranteed to bring sighs of ecstasy from dinner guests!

Eggs are the foundation for these recipes, with the yolks and the whites going their separate ways, to thicken, and to add volume and lightness. When heated, yolks will thicken cream or milk, to make a custard. Whisked whites add lightness and volume to soufflés and mousses. Yolks whisked with sugar become very thick, making them the perfect base for flavourings such as fruit juices and melted chocolate.

Cream adds richness, and when it is whipped it will add volume and lightness, too. Custards can be made with double or single cream, or with milk if you prefer a less rich mixture. Custard made with cream has a smooth velvety texture, which is why it can be served as a dessert in its own right, in the form of Crème brûlée, or Petits Pots de Crème. Bavarois is a classic dessert made with a rich custard, lightened with whipped cream, and set with gelatine. Bavarois, and other creamy mixtures can be set in decorative moulds. Bavarois mixture can also be used as the filling for an elaborate gâteau, or sweet pastry flan case.

Cold soufflés are very light mixtures set high above a soufflé dish, as imitations of hot soufflés.

Making a custard

A custard is easily ruined if the mixture is overheated, and for this reason they are not usually cooked over direct heat, but in a bowl placed over a saucepan of gently simmering hot water. Constant stirring is needed to prevent the mixture overheating in the bottom of the bowl. A slow, even cooking makes a smoother custard. Once thickened, the custard should be strained immediately, through a nylon sieve into a bowl.

Whipping cream

To enable cream to be blended smoothly with the mixture it is being added to, it should be of a similar consistency. Most of the desserts require the cream to be whipped to a soft peak, or until it will only just hold the trail of the whisk.

Use very fresh cream for whipping; the fresher it is, the longer it will take to whisk. If the cream is not fresh, it will thicken with a few turns of the whisk, becoming solid rather than light and airy.

☞

FROZEN PASSION FRUIT SOUFFLÉ (page 67)

It should always be well chilled, and preferably whisked in a chilled mixing bowl.

If cream is over whisked before it is blended with another mixture, it will continue to thicken as it is mixed in, making it very difficult to obtain a smooth mixture. Acid in fruit purée will thicken cream on contact, so it is better to slightly under whisk it when the cream is to be added to a mixture containing a high percentage of acid purée. The same happens when cream is added to fruit juice and wine, as when making a syllabub.

Gelatine

For moulded creams to be turned out, and mousses and soufflés to retain their shape, they must be set with gelatine. Gelatine comes in two forms, powdered and leaf. Leaf gelatine is more difficult to buy these days, so the following recipes all use powdered.

Whether gelatine is to be added to a hot or a cold mixture, it must always be softened in a little cold water first. The gelatine must be sprinkled over the water, not the other way round.

It is then left for a few minutes, until the gelatine has absorbed the water – swelling and becoming opaque. At this stage it can be added to a hot mixture, such as the custard for a bavarois, then stirred until it is melted into the mixture.

Adding gelatine to a cold mixture is a little more difficult. It must be melted first, heating it until it is quite hot – hot enough to sting your little finger.

If cool gelatine is added to a cold mixture, it will set on contact with the mixture setting in fine threads, known as 'roping'. The mixture will not set properly or it will set the mixture too quickly,

before you have a chance to fold in the egg whites or cream; either way, it will taste most unpleasant. Whisking the gelatine into a mixture will blend it in quickly and smoothly.

Whisking egg whites

The airy, sponge-like, texture of a cold soufflé is achieved by the careful addition of egg whites. They must be whisked until stiff, but not dry, to enable them to be mixed in easily.

Gently fold egg whites into a mousse, or soufflé mixture with a large metal spoon, or rubber spatula. Cut through the centre of the mixture, right down to the bottom of the mixing bowl, then bring the mixture up and over itself. Give the bowl a quarter turn, and repeat. Repeat until completely mixed in. Pour into the dish.

Soufflé dishes and moulds

Choose a soufflé dish that is about 5–7 cm (2½–3 inches) deep; the mixture should stand above the dish by up to as much as half the depth of the dish. If you are using a larger quantity of mixture, use a wider dish, rather than a deeper one.

For a cold soufflé to be set above the dish, the dish must have a paper collar put around it. Greaseproof paper or typewriting paper can be used. Cut a length of paper long enough to fit right around the dish, with an overlap. The width of the paper strip should be about 5–6 cm (2–2½ inches) larger than the depth of the soufflé dish. Place the strip around the dish and secure it with a piece of sticky tape.

Moulds, for moulded desserts, should have a clearly defined pattern. Tin-lined copper are usually the best moulds; it is also easier to remove a set mixture from a metal mould than from a thick china, or glass mould. When the mould is dipped into hot water, the heat will penetrate quickly through metal, melting the mixture sufficiently for it to slide out easily. Moulds may be lightly oiled with a little almond oil, but never with a cooking oil as this could taint the cream.

Frozen Passion Fruit Soufflé

A velvety smooth soufflé to make the perfect ending to a dinner party, it should be made the day before. The soufflé can be decorated with whipped cream and pistachio nuts, but as its impressive qualities are in the texture and fresh flavour, it really doesn't need to be dressed-up.

16 passion fruit	600 ml (1 pint) double
6 egg yolks	cream
175 g (6 oz) caster sugar	
	SERVES EIGHT

Prepare a 15 cm (6 inch), 6 cm (2½ inch) deep, soufflé dish as instructed on page 66.

Cut each passion fruit in half and scoop out the flesh and seeds into a nylon sieve placed over a small bowl then press with a spoon to extract all of the juice – about 150 ml (¼ pint).

Put the egg yolks into a large bowl and whisk well, preferably with an electric mixer, until very thick.

Put 60 ml (4 tbsp) of the passion fruit juice into a small saucepan with the caster sugar. Stir over a low heat until the sugar has dissolved, then bring to the boil and boil until the temperature reaches 110°C (230°F) on a sugar thermometer. Whisk the syrup in a steady stream into the egg yolks, then continue whisking until the mixture cools and thickens. Gradually whisk in the remaining passion fruit juice, whisking until the mixture is thick and mousse-like.

Whip the cream until it just holds its shape. Fold the cream into the passion fruit mixture until no trace of white remains. Pour into the prepared soufflé dish, then freeze until firm. Once frozen, cover the top of the soufflé with clingfilm.

To serve, remove the soufflé from the freezer 20–30 minutes before serving and carefully peel off the clingfilm and paper. Serve the soufflé on a doily-lined dish.

Simple Lemon Soufflé

This simple soufflé is the lightest and most refreshing of all cold soufflés and is a perfect palate-freshener.

6 eggs, separated	**Decoration**
175 g (6 oz) caster sugar	150 ml (¼ pint) double
finely grated rind and	cream
juice of 3 large lemons	10 ml (2 tsp) caster sugar
27.5 ml (5½ tsp)	finely grated lemon rind
powdered gelatine	
60 ml (4 tbsp) water	SERVES SIX

Prepare a 15 cm (6 inch), 6 cm (2½ inch) deep, soufflé dish as instructed on page 66.

Whisk the egg yolks, caster sugar and lemon rind in a large bowl, until very thick, and the mixture holds the trail of a whisk for at least 5 seconds. Gradually whisk in the strained lemon juice.

Sprinkle the gelatine over the water in a small bowl and leave to soften for 2 minutes. Stand in a pan of hot water and stir until dissolved and hot.

Whisk the egg whites until stiff, but not dry. Whisk the gelatine into the lemon mixture, then carefully fold in the egg whites until no trace of white remains.

Pour the soufflé mixture into the prepared dish, then cut through the surface of the soufflé with a small pointed knife, to level. Chill until set.

Whip the cream with the caster sugar until it is just thick enough to pipe, then spoon into a piping bag fitted with a small star nozzle. Carefully peel off the paper collar from the soufflé. Decorate with rosettes of cream, then sprinkle with lemon rind.

Chocolate and Orange Mousse

Serve this mousse in tall glasses. It is very rich, so choose it as a dessert for a menu, where the main courses are not rich.

175 g (6 oz) plain	15 g (½ oz) icing sugar
chocolate	15–30 (1–2 tbsp) Grand
30 ml (2 tbsp) orange	Marnier, or brandy
juice	
finely grated rind of 1	**Decoration**
orange	grated chocolate curls
40 g (1½ oz) unsalted	finely grated orange rind
butter	
4 eggs, separated	SERVES SIX
225 ml (8 fl oz) double	
cream	

Break up the chocolate and put in a large bowl with the orange juice and rind. Set the bowl over a saucepan of hot water until the chocolate melts, stirring frequently. Add the butter, a little at a time, then stir in the egg yolks. Remove the bowl from the heat.

Whisk the egg whites until stiff, but not dry, then fold them into the chocolate mixture. Divide the mixture between six tall glasses and chill until set.

Whip the cream with the icing sugar and the Grand Marnier until it just holds soft peaks. Spoon the cream in whirls on top of the mousse. Decorate with chocolate curls and grated orange rind. Serve well chilled.

STRAWBERRY BAVAROIS (page 74)

Raspberry Soufflé

Frozen raspberries may be used when fresh ones are not available. Other purées, such as strawberry, apricot, blackberry, blackcurrant, blueberry or mango may be used instead of raspberry.

225 g (8 oz) raspberries
6 eggs, separated
100 g (4 oz) caster sugar
22.5 ml (1½ tbsp) powdered gelatine
60 ml (4 tbsp) water
150 ml (¼ pint) double cream

Decoration
150 ml (¼ pint) double cream, whipped
fresh raspberries

SERVES SIX TO EIGHT

Prepare a 15 cm (6 inch), 6 cm (2½ inch) deep, soufflé dish as instructed on page 66. Press the raspberries through a nylon sieve to make a purée.

Whisk the egg yolks and sugar in a large bowl, until pale and thick and the mixture holds the trail of a whisk for at least 5 seconds. Whisk in the purée.

Sprinkle the gelatine over the water in a small bowl and leave to soften for 2 minutes. Stand in a saucepan of hot water and stir until dissolved and very hot.

Whip the cream until it will hold soft peaks. Whisk the egg whites until stiff, but not dry.

Whisk the gelatine into the raspberry mixture. Fold in the cream, then the egg whites. Pour the mixture into the prepared soufflé dish and level the surface. Chill until set.

Carefully peel off the paper from the soufflé. Decorate the top of the soufflé with piped cream and fresh raspberries.

Crème Brûlée

Crème brûlée is a speciality of Trinity College, Cambridge. The split vanilla bean used for flavouring gives the custard a speckled appearance; if preferred, vanilla essence can be used instead.

8 egg yolks
50 g (2 oz) caster sugar
600 ml (1 pint) double cream

1 vanilla bean, split lengthways

SERVES FOUR TO SIX

Put the egg yolks into a mixing bowl with 25 g (1 oz) of the caster sugar and whisk very lightly together.

Put the cream into a saucepan with the vanilla bean and heat gently until almost boiling. Gently whisk the cream into the egg yolks.

Set the bowl of custard over a saucepan of hot water and cook, stirring, until the custard becomes thick. Immediately, strain the custard through a nylon sieve into a heatproof serving dish, about 20 cm (8 inch) diameter and 2.5 cm (1 inch) deep. Allow the custard to cool, then chill in the refrigerator, preferably overnight, until set.

About 2 hours before serving, remove the custard from the refrigerator and sprinkle the surface with the remaining caster sugar, making sure that it forms a very even layer. Allow to stand for about 10 minutes, then cook under a hot grill until the sugar dissolves and turns a golden caramel colour. Cool, then chill before serving.

Blackberry Mousse

This mousse is made without gelatine and must be chilled thoroughly before serving. It can also be made with raspberries or strawberries.

225 g (8 oz) fresh or
  frozen blackberries
2 eggs, separated
50 g (2 oz) caster sugar
300 ml (½ pint) double
  cream

a few blackberries, with
  leaves if possible, to
  decorate

SERVES SIX

Press the blackberries through a nylon sieve to make a purée, about 225 ml (8 fl oz).

Whisk the egg yolks in a large mixing bowl with the caster sugar until very thick, then whisk in the blackberry purée.

Whip the cream until thick enough to leave a trial on the surface when the whisk is lifted, then fold into the blackberry mixture. Continue to whisk until the mixture will form a heavy trial. Whisk the egg whites until they stand in soft peaks, then fold into the blackberry mixture.

Spoon the blackberry mousse into six serving glasses and chill for about 2 hours. Serve decorated with fresh blackberries and their leaves, hung in clusters over the sides of the glasses.

Old English Syllabub

Bring out the full fragrance of the spices by grinding them just before you use them. Decorate the syllabub with fresh edible flower petals such as nasturtium, geranium, and rose, or with borage flowers.

1 clove
1 allspice
2.5 cm (1 inch) piece of
  cinnamon stick
a little freshly grated
  nutmeg
50 g (2 oz) caster sugar
finely grated rind and
  juice of 1 lemon

90 ml (6 tbsp) pale cream
  sherry
300 ml (½ pint) double
  cream
24 ratafias

SERVES FOUR

Put the clove, allspice and cinnamon stick into a small mortar and grind very finely, then sift through a fine sieve.

Put the ground spices, nutmeg, sugar, lemon rind, and strained lemon juice into a bowl with the sherry. Stir well until the sugar dissolves, then cover and leave to stand for 1 hour.

Strain the sherry mixture through a fine nylon sieve into a clean bowl. Pour in the cream in a steady stream, whisking all the time. Whip the cream until it is just thick enough to hold the trail of a whisk.

Place four ratafias in each of four serving glasses, then fill each glass with the spicy syllabub. Chill for about 1 hour. Decorate with the remaining ratafias and a few fresh flower petals.

Coeurs à la Crème

These pretty heart-shaped creams are traditionally served with wild strawberries, but they can also be served with other fresh, sharp-flavoured fruits such as raspberries, strawberries or sliced kiwi fruit.

275 g (10 oz) curd or ricotta cheese
25 g (1 oz) caster sugar
finely grated rind of 1 lemon
finely grated rind of 1 orange
300 ml (½ pint) double cream
2 egg whites

Decoration
150 ml (¼ pint) double cream
wild strawberries, raspberries or kiwi fruit, to serve

SERVES SIX

Rinse 12 pieces of muslin in water and wring out well. Line six coeur à la crème moulds with a double layer of muslin, pressing it well into the corners, allowing the muslin to overhang the edges.

Sieve the cheese through a nylon sieve into a bowl, then mix in the sugar and the rind.

Whip the cream until it will hold soft peaks. Whisk the egg whites until stiff, but not dry. Fold the cream into the cheese, then fold in the whites.

Spoon the cheese mixture into the moulds, then bring the muslin up and over the filling. Place on a plate and leave to drain overnight in the fridge.

Discard the liquid and remove the clingfilm. Invert the creams on to individual serving plates and gently remove the muslin. Pour the double cream evenly over the creams, then decorate with the chosen fruit.

Lime Syllabub

Serve this well-flavoured syllabub with langues de chat biscuits. Lemon may be used instead of lime, but if so, use only one.

thinly pared rind and juice of 3 limes
150 ml (¼ pint) white wine
30 ml (2 tbsp) brandy
75 g (3 oz) caster sugar

300 ml (½ pint) double cream
lime twists, to decorate

SERVES FOUR TO SIX

Put the lime rind and juice, white wine, brandy and caster sugar into a bowl. Stir well until the sugar has dissolved, then cover and leave to stand for about 2 hours.

Remove the rind from the wine with a slotted spoon and discard. Pour the cream into the wine in a continuous stream, stirring with a whisk. Whip the cream until thick and it holds the trail of a whisk, then pour into serving glasses and chill. Serve decorated with lime twists.

Petits Pots de Crème – Caramel

Care must be taken when making the caramel; should it become too dark it will give the cream a bitter flavour. You can use all milk instead of milk and cream, if preferred.

75 g (3 oz) granulated sugar	1 whole egg
45 ml (3 tbsp) water	300 ml (½ pint) single cream
300 ml (½ pint) milk	
5 egg yolks	SERVES SIX TO EIGHT

Put the sugar into a heavy-based saucepan with the water and heat gently until the sugar has dissolved.

Bring the sugar syrup to the boil and boil until it turns a light brown caramel colour, then immediately plunge the base of the saucepan into cold water to stop the caramel cooking and darkening further. Carefully pour in the milk, then heat gently until the caramel dissolves into the milk.

Lightly whisk the egg yolks and whole egg together. Stir in the cream, and the caramel-flavoured milk. Strain the mixture through a nylon sieve into eight 75 ml (3 fl oz) petit pots, or six 100 ml (4 fl oz) soufflé dishes. Cover with lids or small rounds of aluminium foil.

Stand the dishes on a trivet in a large, wide saucepan, and add enough boiling water to come about halfway up the sides of the dishes. Cover the pan with a lid, then steam the creams over a gentle heat for 15–20 minutes until they are very lightly set. Allow to cool. Chill well before serving.

Petits Pots de Crème – Chocolate

If you do not have the special little china pots for making this rich cream, you can use small soufflé dishes. A less rich cream can be made by using milk instead of cream.

600 ml (1 pint) single cream	1 whole egg
2.5 ml (½ tsp) vanilla essence	25 g (1 oz) caster sugar
175 g (6 oz) plain chocolate, broken into small pieces	SERVES SIX TO EIGHT
5 egg yolks	

Put the cream, vanilla essence and the chocolate into a saucepan and heat gently, stirring, until the chocolate melts and the mixture becomes smooth.

Lightly mix the egg yolks, whole egg and the caster sugar together, then stir in the chocolate cream. Strain the mixture through a nylon sieve into eight 75 ml (3 fl oz) petit pots, or six 100 ml (4 fl oz) soufflé dishes. Cover the petit pots with lids or small rounds of aluminium foil; cover the soufflé dishes with aluminium foil.

Stand the dishes on a trivet in a large, wide saucepan, and add enough boiling water to come about halfway up the sides of the dishes. Cover the pan with a lid, then stream the creams over a gently heat for 15–20 minutes until they are very lightly set. Remove from the pan and allow to cool. Chill well before serving.

Vanilla Bavarian Ring

This vanilla-flavoured bavarois is set in a ring mould and decorated with chocolate leaves, but it can be set in any pretty mould and decorated with cherries or grapes dipped in caramel; piped chocolate scrolls; fresh fruits, or edible flower petals.

15 ml (1 tbsp) powdered
  gelatine
45 ml (3 tbsp) water
6 egg yolks
50 g (2 oz) caster sugar
300 ml (½ pint) single
  cream
5 ml (1 tsp) vanilla
  essence
300 ml (½ pint) double
  cream

Decoration
75 g (3 oz) plain chocolate
12 rose leaves
150 ml (¼ pint) crème
  Chantilly (see page 94)

SERVES SIX

Sprinkle the gelatine over the water and leave to soften while making the custard.

Lightly whisk the egg yolks and the caster sugar together in a bowl. Bring the single cream and the vanilla essence almost to the boil, then whisk into the egg yolks. Set the bowl over a saucepan of hot water and cook the custard, stirring, until it thickens enough to coat the back of the spoon (alternatively, cook in a microwave oven on full power for 2–2½ minutes, stirring every 30 seconds with a wire whisk).

Strain the custard through a nylon sieve into a clean bowl and add the gelatine. Stir until it is completely dissolved. Allow the custard to cool, stirring frequently to prevent a skin forming.

Whip the cream until it will just hold soft peaks, then fold the custard and the cream together. Pour into a 1.1 litre (2 pint) ring mould. Chill until set.

Meanwhile, make the decoration. Melt the chocolate and dip the underside of the rose leaves into the chocolate. Leave to set, then remove leaves.

To unmould the bavarois, quickly dip the mould, right up to the rim, into hot water. Place a serving plate on top, then invert the mould.

Whip the crème Chantilly until thick enough to pipe, then fill a piping bag fitted with a star nozzle. Pipe the cream around the base of the mould, then decorate with the chocolate leaves.

Strawberry Bavarois

It is essential to use really well-flavoured strawberries for this bavarois – frozen strawberries may be used, but only as a last resort.

about 350 g (12 oz) fresh
  strawberries
22.5 ml (1½ tbsp)
  powdered gelatine
60 ml (4 tbsp) water
6 egg yolks
50 g (2 oz) caster sugar
300 ml (½ pint) milk
300 ml (½ pint) double
  cream

Strawberry sauce
225 g (8 oz) fresh
  strawberries

50 g (2 oz) caster sugar
15 ml (1 tbsp) framboise,
  optional

Decoration
150 ml (¼ pint) double
  cream, whipped
fresh strawberries

SERVES SIX TO EIGHT

Press the strawberries through a very fine nylon sieve to make a purée, about 300 ml (½ pint).

Sprinkle the gelatine over the water in a small bowl and leave to soften while making the custard.

Lightly whisk the egg yolks and the caster sugar together. Bring the milk almost to the boil, then whisk it into the egg yolks. Set the bowl over a saucepan of hot water, and cook the custard, stirring, until it thickens enough to coat the back of the spoon (alternatively, cook in a microwave oven on full power for 2½–3 minutes, stirring every 30 seconds with a wire whisk).

Strain the custard through a nylon sieve into a clean bowl and add the gelatine, stirring until it is completely dissolved. Set the custard aside until cold, but not set, stirring to prevent a skin forming.

Whip the cream until it will just hold soft peaks. Stir the strawberry purée into the custard, then gently fold in the whipped cream. Pour the mixture into a 1.4 litre (2½ pint) mould. Chill until set.

Meanwhile, make the sauce, slice the strawberries and put them into a bowl. Sprinkle with the sugar and the liqueur, if using, cover and leave to stand for about 1 hour, then press through a nylon sieve to form a purée. Pour into a serving jug and chill.

To unmould the bavarois, quickly dip the mould, right up to the rim, into hot water. Place a serving plate on top, then invert the mould and the plate together, giving the mould a sharp shake to free the bavarois. Decorate with whipped cream and fresh strawberries. Serve the bavarois with the chilled strawberry sauce.

Meringues

THE MOST frequently asked cookery question must be 'Why can't I make meringue?' A fact that would surely sadden its Swiss creator, a pastry chef called Gasparini, who was said to have created it as long ago as 1720.

Meringue can be used to make simple piped shells that can be dipped into chocolate, sprinkled with nuts, or sandwiched together with flavourful creams. It makes a fluffy, light topping for pies and puddings; elaborate gâteaux; nests and baskets for filling with fruits and creams; or it can become a grand presentation in the form of a meringue Croquembouche.

◆ Making Meringue ◆

The egg whites must be whisked in a clean bowl until they are very stiff, and will hold an unwavering peak on the end of the whisk.

The sugar can be added in two ways. Half the sugar can be whisked in, then the remaining half folded in, taking care not to overfold and break down the egg whites. This meringue can be piped, but it is better for spooning on top of pies, or for baked Alaska. Alternatively, all the sugar may be whisked in, a little at a time, whisking well between each addition. This makes a very smooth, shiny meringue for piping.

Meringue cuite is made by putting the unwhisked whites and caster, or icing sugar into a large mixing bowl, then whisking them over gently simmering water until they become stiff and thick. As soon as the mixture becomes thick, the bowl should be removed from the heat, and the meringue whisked until it will hold stiff peaks. This meringue has a smooth texture and a wonderful gloss. It is perfect for piping as it keeps a clearly defined shape. However, care must be taken not to overheat the meringue when whisking, or it will form a frothy, cooked egg texture.

Once made, meringue should be used immediately. If it is left for any length of time it will collapse, become watery, and be unusable. Meringue can be baked in the oven at a very low temperature for a long time to completely dry out (as for shells, discs, and nests) or it can be baked at a higher temperature for a short time.

◆ Drying Meringues ◆

How meringues are cooked is very much a personal choice, but it seems that everyone's ideal is to dry them out so that they remain pure white. This is for visual effect only. Creamy coloured meringues with a slightly soft centre have a better flavour, but they don't look quite so attractive.

For meringues to remain pure white, they need to be left in an oven set at its lowest possible setting, for several hours, even overnight in some cases. Check from time-to-time to make sure that they are not colouring.

LEMON MERINGUE PIE (page 79)

Meringue Medley

Made with meringue cuite, these little meringues are favourites with adults and children alike. Serve with morning coffee, or afternoon tea.

6 egg whites	25 g (1 oz) pecans,
350 g (12 oz) caster sugar	walnuts, or hazelnuts,
15 ml (1 tbsp) finely	finely chopped
chopped pistachio nuts	15 ml (1 tbsp) raspberry
300 ml (½ pint) double	purée
cream	75 g (3 oz) plain
15 ml (1 tbsp) Grand	chocolate, melted
Marnier	

MAKES FORTY-FOUR SMALL MERINGUES

Line several baking sheets with non-stick baking paper cut to fit the sheets.

Put the egg whites and caster sugar together in a large bowl over a large saucepan of hot water and whisk until very stiff and shiny. Remove from the heat and continue whisking until the meringue will hold unwavering peaks – on no account let the meringue become too hot.

Fill a large piping bag, fitted with a large star nozzle, with meringue and pipe out as follows:–

To make whirls: pipe 24 whirls of meringue on the lined baking sheets, about 4 cm (1½ inches) in diameter.

To make oblong spirals: pipe the meringue in a spiral fashion to make 24 spirals about 7.5 cm (3 inches) long. Or, if you find it easier, pipe a joined line of shells to the same length.

To make pistachio fingers: simply pipe 20 straight lines of meringue about 7.5 cm (3 inches) long on the baking sheets, then sprinkle with chopped pistachio nuts.

Bake the meringues at 140°C (275°F) mark 1 for 2–2½ hours, or until completely dried out. Change the trays around in the oven during cooking, to ensure that they all dry evenly. Allow the meringues to cool, then remove from the paper and complete as follows or, store in an airtight tin until required.

Whirls: whisk 150 ml (¼ pint) of the double cream with the Grand Marnier until it will hold soft peaks, then fold in the chopped nuts. Sandwich the meringues together, in pairs, with the nut cream, then place in small paper cases for serving.

Spirals: whisk the remaining cream until thick, then fold in the raspberry purée. Put the cream into a piping bag fitted with a large star nozzle. Sandwich the meringues together, in pairs, with piped cream. Put the meringues into small paper cases for serving.

Pistachio fingers: dip the base of each meringue in the melted chocolate to coat it evenly, removing excess chocolate by gently pulling the meringue across the back of a knife. Place on greaseproof paper until set.

Lemon Meringue Pie

Lemon meringue pie comes in various forms.
This delicious version has a lemon filling which
is cool, smooth and tangy.

1 quantity pâte sucrée (see page 92)	50–75 g (2–3 oz) caster sugar
lightly whipped cream, to serve	3 egg yolks
	Meringue
Filling	3 egg whites
rind and juice of 4 large lemons	175 g (6 oz) caster sugar
600ml (1 pint) water	SERVES SIX TO EIGHT
65 g (2½ oz) cornflour	

Roll out the pâte sucrée on a lightly floured surface to a round 2.5 cm (1 inch) larger than a 23 cm (9 inch) fluted flan tin. Line the dish with the pastry, pressing it well into the flutes. Trim the edge, then prick the pastry well, all over, with a fork. Chill for 30 minutes, then bake blind at 220°C (425°F) mark 7 for 25–30 minutes, until cooked and lightly browned. Allow to cool. Leave the oven on.

Meanwhile, prepare the filling, put the lemon rind in a saucepan with the water, bring to the boil, then remove from the heat, cover, and leave to stand for at least 30 minutes.

Remove all of the lemon rind from the pan, then stir in the lemon juice. Blend the cornflour with a little of the lemon liquid to form a smooth paste, pour it into the pan and stir well. Bring the lemon mixture to the boil, stirring continuously. Reduce the heat and continue cooking until every trace of raw cornflour disappears, and the mixture has thickened. Stir in the sugar to taste, adding a little more if liked, then beat in the egg yolks. Pour the lemon filling into the pastry case.

To make the meringue, whisk the egg whites until stiff, but not dry, then gradually whisk in the sugar, adding a little at a time and whisking well between each addition, until the meringue is very stiff and shiny. Put the meringue into a large piping bag fitted with a large star nozzle, then pipe it attractively on top of the lemon filling.

Alternatively, spoon the meringue on to the filling and shape it into swirls with a palette knife. Bake for 5–10 minutes until the meringue is very lightly browned. Remove the pie from the oven and allow to cool, then refrigerate until quite cold. Serve with lightly whipped cream.

Swiss Flan

The tip of every meringue star in this dessert is dotted with a bead of redcurrant jelly to give a jewelled effect. A little skill with a piping bag is needed as each star must have a clean point, to enable it to be dotted with jelly.

1 quantity of pâte sucrée (see page 92)	*Meringue*
	3 egg whites
	175 g (6 oz) caster sugar
Filling	30 ml (2 tbsp) redcurrant
225 g (8 oz) granulated sugar	jelly or raspberry seedless jam
juice of 1 lemon, strained	
150 ml (¼ pint) water	SERVES SIX TO EIGHT
900 g (2 lb) dessert apples	

Roll the pâte sucrée out on a lightly floured surface to a round 2.5 cm (1 inch) larger than a 23 cm (9 inch) fluted flan tin. Line the tin with the pastry, pressing it well into the flutes. Trim the edge, then prick the pastry well, all over, with a fork. Chill for 30 minutes.

Bake blind at 220°C (425°F) mark 7 for 20–25 minutes until cooked, and lightly browned. Allow to cool. Reduce the oven temperature to 140°C (275°F) mark 1.

To make the filling, put the sugar and lemon juice into a wide saucepan with the water. Heat gently until the sugar has dissolved, then bring to the boil gently for 5 minutes. Peel, quarter, core and slice the apples, cutting the slices about 0.5 cm (¼ inch) thick. Add the apple slices, in batches, to the sugar syrup and poach until just tender. Lift out with a slotted spoon and drain well on absorbent kitchen paper.

Leaving the pastry case in the flan tin, arrange the apple slices neatly inside the flan case.

Put the egg whites and the caster sugar for the meringue into a bowl, then place over a pan of hot water, whisk until stiff, remove from the heat and continue whisking until the meringue forms unwavering peaks. Put into a piping bag fitted with a large star nozzle, then pipe stars over the top of the apple-filled flan, making sure that each star is finished with a clean point. Continue to pipe the meringue, in decreasing circles, until it builds up to a point.

Bake for 1 hour until the meringue is set, but not browned – it must remain as white as possible.

Put the redcurrant jelly into a small paper piping bag and cut a small hole in the bottom of the bag. Pipe a small bead of jelly on the tip of every meringue star. Serve the flan warm or cold.

SWISS FLAN (above)

Meringue and Ganache Gâteau

This very rich gâteau makes a lovely party-time special.

---

4 egg whites	30–45 ml (2–3 tbsp)
225 g (8 oz) caster sugar	Grand Marnier, brandy
350 g (12 oz) plain	or rum
chocolate	icing sugar for sifting
475 ml (16 fl oz) double	
cream	SERVES FOURTEEN TO
	SIXTEEN

Line four baking sheets with non-stick baking paper. Draw a 20.5 cm (8 inch) circle in the centre of each sheet of paper.

Whisk the egg whites until stiff, but not dry, then gradually whisk in the caster sugar, a little at a time, whisking well until the meringue is very stiff and shiny. Divide the meringue equally between the four baking sheets, then spread evenly to form neat rounds. Bake at 140°C (275°F) mark 1 for 1–1¼ hours until dry, swapping over the baking sheets during cooking to ensure that they dry out evenly. Cool.

Meanwhile, break the chocolate into small pieces and put into a large saucepan with the double cream. Heat gently, stirring, until the chocolate melts and blends with the cream to form a smooth rich cream; do not allow to boil.

Pour the cream into a mixing bowl and leave to cool, stirring frequently to prevent a skin forming. When the chocolate cream is cold, add the Grand Marnier and whisk well until light and fluffy – do not overwhisk as the cream will turn buttery.

Place one of the meringue layers on a flat serving plate, then spread with a generous layer of the whipped chocolate cream. Continue until the meringue rounds are sandwiched together.

Spread the remaining chocolate cream all over the meringue to cover completely. Mark the cream into swirls with a palette knife. Sift icing sugar lightly over the gâteau. Refrigerate the gâteau until it is slightly chilled, but do not let the chocolate cream set too hard. Serve the gâteau still slightly chilled, so the chocolate cream is still firm.

Hazelnut Meringue Gâteau

This simple gâteau is perfect for the novice meringue-maker. The sharp flavour of the raspberries contrasts well with the nutty meringue.

---

3 egg whites	icing sugar for sifting
175 g (6 oz) caster sugar	finely chopped pistachio
50 g (2 oz) hazelnuts,	nuts for sprinkling
skinned, toasted and	
finely chopped	SERVES SIX TO EIGHT
300 ml (½ pint) double	
cream	
350 g (12 oz) fresh	
raspberries, hulled	

Line two baking sheets with non-stick baking paper, then draw a 20.5 cm (8 inch) circle on each one.

Whisk the egg whites until they are very stiff, but not dry. Adding just a little sugar at a time, gradually whisk the caster sugar into the egg whites, whisking well between each addition until the meringue is stiff and very shiny. Carefully fold in the chopped hazelnuts.

Divide the meringue equally between the two baking sheets, then spread neatly into rounds. With a palette knife, mark the top of one of the rounds into swirls – this will be the top meringue. Bake at 140°C (275°F) mark 1 for about 1½ hours until dry. Turn the oven off, and allow the meringues to cool in the oven.

Whip the cream until it will hold soft peaks. Carefully remove the meringues from the baking paper. Place the smooth meringue round on a large flat serving plate, then spread with the cream. Arrange the raspberries on top of the cream, then place the second meringue on top. Sift icing sugar over the top of the gâteau, and sprinkle with finely chopped pistachio nuts. Serve the gâteau as soon as possible as a dessert.

Tropical Pavlova

The secret of a successful Pavlova is not to remove it from the oven until it is cold – if taken out of the oven while still hot, the sudden change in temperature will cause it to crack.

4 egg whites
3.75 ml (¾ tsp) cream of tartar
225 g (8 oz) caster sugar
5 ml (1 tsp) white vinegar
5 ml (1 tsp) vanilla essence
10 ml (2 tsp) cornflour

Decoration
450 ml (¾ pint) double cream

5 ml (1 tsp) vanilla essence
1 ripe mango, peeled and diced
2 kiwi fruits, peeled and sliced
2 slices of fresh pineapple, peeled, cored and diced

SERVES SIX TO EIGHT

Line a large baking sheet with non-stick baking paper. Whisk the egg whites with the cream of tartar until stiff, but not dry. Gradually whisk in the caster sugar, then quickly whisk in the vinegar, vanilla essence and cornflour.

Spoon the meringue into the centre of the lined baking sheet. Using a large palette knife, spread the meringue to form a smooth oval shape, about 23 cm (9 inches) long and 4 cm (1½ inches) deep. Bake at 140°C (275°F) mark 1 for 1¼ hours, turn the heat off and leave the meringue in the oven until quite cold.

Transfer the meringue to a serving plate, carefully peeling off the paper. Whip the cream with the vanilla essence until stiff, then spoon into a piping bag fitted with a medium-sized star nozzle. Pipe shells of cream around the top edge of the Pavlova. Pipe a second ring of cream, leaving a gap between the rings. Fill the gap with the prepared fruits. (If preferred, the cream may be spread on top of the Pavlova, with the fruits arranged in the centre.)

Meringue Nests

Once these little nests have been well dried out they may be stored in an airtight tin almost indefinitely, making them invaluable as a stand-by in the store cupboard, for instant desserts and unexpected visitors. This recipe gives two alternative fillings (each enough to fill 12 nests), but they can be more simply filled with whipped cream and fruit, or with ice cream.

5 egg whites	175 g (6 oz) curd cheese
275 g (10 oz) caster sugar	150 ml (¼ pint) double cream
Cranberry filling	
20 g (¾ oz) custard powder	*Chestnut filling*
300 ml (½ pint) milk	450 ml (¾ pint) double cream
15 ml (1 tbsp) caster sugar	5 ml (1 tsp) vanilla essence
225 g (8 oz) cranberries or blueberries	500 g (1 lb) can sweetened chestnut purée
100 g (4 oz) granulated sugar	grated chocolate curls, to decorate
60 ml (4 tbsp) water	
10 ml (2 tsp) arrowroot	

MAKES TWELVE NESTS

Line two baking sheets with non-stick baking paper. Draw twelve 10 cm (4 inch) circles on the paper.

Whisk the egg whites until they are very stiff, but not dry, then gradually whisk in the caster sugar a little at a time, whisking well between each addition, until the meringue is very stiff and shiny.

Put the meringue into a large piping bag fitted with a medium-sized star nozzle. Fill in each drawn circle on the baking paper, with a continuous spiral of meringue. Pipe stars of meringue around the edge of each meringue base to form a little wall. Bake at 100°C (200°F) mark Low for 4–5 hours. Turn the oven off and leave the meringues until cool.

For cranberry filled nests, blend the custard powder with the caster sugar and a little of the milk to form a smooth paste. Bring the remaining milk to the boil, then stir it into the custard mixture. Return the custard to the saucepan and cook over a low heat, stirring, until the custard thickens. Pour the custard into a clean bowl, then cover the surface closely with clingfilm to prevent a skin forming. Allow to cool, then refrigerate until quite cold.

Put the cranberries into a saucepan with the granulated sugar and water, cover and cook gently for about 15 minutes until the cranberries are softened. Blend the arrowroot with a little cold water to form a smooth paste, then stir into the cranberries. Bring to the boil, stirring until the mixture thickens and clears. Pour into a small bowl, cover the surface closely with clingfilm to prevent a skin forming, allow to cool, then refrigerate until well chilled.

Beat the curd cheese until it is soft and smooth. Whip the cream until it will hold soft peaks. Whisk the cold custard until it is very smooth, mix with the curd cheese, then fold in the cream. Divide the custard mixture between the meringue nests, then spoon the cranberries on top. Serve immediately, or chill until ready to serve.

For chestnut filled nests, whip the cream with the vanilla essence until it is just thick enough to pipe, then put it into a piping bag fitted with a medium-sized star nozzle.

Spoon the chestnut purée into the meringue nests, then pipe the cream in whirls on top. If preferred, the cream may be spooned on top. Sprinkle chocolate curls over the cream. Serve immediately, or chill until ready to serve.

HAZELNUT MERINGUE GÂTEAU (page 82)

Basic Recipes

Génoise

This very light sponge cake is the foundation for many gâteaux, but it can also be used to make quick cakes for afternoon tea, or for desserts. The amount of flour and butter used to eggs varies from one recipe to another; the recipe below uses half butter to flour. It can be made with up to an equal quantity of butter to flour, but this will make a firmer sponge.

Although Génoise can be used on the same day it is made, it is much easier to handle, and will cut better, if it is kept for a day, well wrapped in clingfilm, or aluminium foil before using. Génoise becomes more moist with keeping, and will keep for two or three days.

The eggs and sugar are normally whisked in a bowl over a saucepan of gently simmering water with a balloon or rotary whisk, or hand held electric mixer – but if you have a free standing mixer, whisking over hot water is unnecessary.

To achieve a very light sponge, use a large metal spoon or a rubber spatula to fold in the flour as these enable you to cut cleanly through the whisked egg mixture without losing any of the air. Always make sure that the melted butter is quite cool before adding it to the sponge mixture, if it is too hot it will deflate the mixture. As soon as the last trace of butter disappears, pour the mixture into a prepared tin and bake immediately – if the mixture is left to stand for any length of time it will simply collapse and be unusable.

SURPRISINGLY few pieces of special equipment are needed to create wonderful cakes and pastries. Large heavy baking sheets are essential, as is a piping bag with a good selection of plain and star nozzles. A torten ring is most useful, and is a good buy if you don't already have one. This is a deep metal ring that can be expanded, or reduced, to whatever size you wish. It can also be used as a mould for baking sponge cakes, by placing it on a foil-lined baking sheet, with the foil pleated up around the ring to prevent the mixture seeping out. But the rings are particularly useful for assembling layered cakes. The ring enables the cake to be trimmed to an exact size, and it keeps the layers held firmly together whilst being assembled, to give a perfect shape when finished. Springform tins are useful and should have a good solid base; some have very thin bases that become very wavy, which in turn can make cakes very uneven. The measurements for all of the tins and dishes used throughout this book are taken across the top.

Non-stick baking paper, and greaseproof paper are both essential for lining tins, and for making disposable paper piping bags. Several sizes of palette knife with very flexible blades are useful.

6 eggs
175 g (6 oz) caster sugar
175 g (6 oz) plain flour

75 g (3 oz) unsalted
butter, melted and
cooled

MAKES A 25 cm (10 inch)
CAKE

Butter and lightly flour a 25 cm (10 inch) round
springform tin. Line the base with a round of
greaseproof paper.

Put the eggs and caster sugar into a large bowl,
place over a saucepan of hot water and whisk well
until the mixture becomes very thick, and very light
in colour. Remove from the heat and whisk until
cold, and thick enough to leave a trail on the surface
when the whisk is lifted. Alternatively, whisk the
eggs and sugar together in a large electric mixer until
they hold a trail almost indefinitely.

Sift the flour into a bowl, then gradually fold into
the whisked mixture, cutting through and folding
the mixture over to incorporate the flour, turning the
bowl each time you cut through the mixture. Fold in
the cooled butter a little at a time, taking care not to
over mix or the mixture will collapse.

Pour the mixture into the prepared tin, tapping
the tin gently to level the mixture. Bake at 180°C
(350°F) mark 4 for 40–45 minutes until the sponge is
well risen, firm to the touch, and has shrunk very
slightly away from the side of the tin. Cool the
sponge in the tin for about 10 minutes, then transfer
to a wire rack to cool completely.

Biscuit de Savoie

*This light, fatless sponge is made with potato
flour. As with Génoise, the sponge will contract
as it cools. If it dips in the centre, simply trim
the sides to level.*

50 g (2 oz) potato flour
50 g (2 oz) plain flour
5 eggs, separated
175 g (6 oz) caster sugar

finely grated rind of 1
lemon

MAKES A 25 cm (10 inch)
CAKE

Butter and lightly flour a 25 cm (10 inch) round
springform tin. Line the base with a round of
greaseproof paper.

Sift the potato flour and the plain flour together
twice. Whisk the egg yolks with three-quarters of the
caster sugar and lemon rind in a large mixing bowl
until they are very thick.

Whisk the egg whites until stiff, but not dry, then
gradually whisk in the remaining caster sugar,
whisking until very shiny. Carefully fold the sifted
flours into the egg yolk mixture, then gradually fold
in the egg whites.

Pour the sponge mixture into the prepared tin and
bake at 180°C (350°F) mark 4 for 40–45 minutes until
very well risen, and a wooden cocktail stick or
skewer inserted in the centre of the sponge comes
out clean. Allow the sponge to cool in the tin for 10
minutes, then transfer to a wire rack to cool
completely.

Shortcrust Pastry

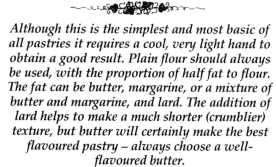

Although this is the simplest and most basic of all pastries it requires a cool, very light hand to obtain a good result. Plain flour should always be used, with the proportion of half fat to flour. The fat can be butter, margarine, or a mixture of butter and margarine, and lard. The addition of lard helps to make a much shorter (crumblier) texture, but butter will certainly make the best flavoured pastry – always choose a well-flavoured butter.

This pastry is bound together with chilled water and care must be taken not to add too much, or too little. If the pastry is too wet, it will be sticky to handle and tough to eat. If it is too dry, it will crumble and be impossible to roll out. As flours vary in strength (the gluten content) from one brand to another, a little more or a little less water may be necessary to bind the mixture to the right consistency. The addition of sugar improves the flavour.

175 g (6 oz) plain flour	75 g (3 oz) butter, cubed
pinch of salt	30 ml (2 tbsp) chilled
15 ml (1 tbsp) caster sugar	water

Sift the flour, salt and sugar into a bowl. Rub in the butter until the mixture resembles fine breadcrumbs.

Make a well in the centre of the rubbed-in mixture, add the water and mix together with a round-bladed knife to form a dough that is firm and will leave the bowl quite clean. Turn the dough on to a lightly floured surface and knead it just for a few seconds to smooth. Use as directed.

Rich Shortcrust Pastry

This richer version of shortcrust pastry has a higher proportion of fat (which should be all butter or margarine) and an added egg yolk. It may also be made with a whole egg, instead of egg yolk and water. The pastry keeps well, and is excellent for pies, tarts or flans that are to be eaten cold.

225 g (8 oz) plain flour	1 egg yolk
pinch of salt	30 ml (2 tbsp) chilled
15 ml (1 tbsp) caster sugar	water
150 g (5 oz) butter, cubed	

Sift the flour, salt and sugar into a bowl. Rub in the butter until the mixture resembles breadcrumbs.

Mix the egg yolk and water together (this ensures an evenly coloured pastry; when added separately the pastry can become streaky in appearance), add to the dough and mix lightly. Knead on a lightly floured surface for a few seconds until smooth.

Puff Pastry

Used for famous gâteaux such as Pithiviers, mille-feuilles and jalousie, as well as numerous other large and small sweet pastries, this is one of the richest, and lightest pastries. It contains an equal amount of butter to flour, and its lightness is achieved by the clever layering of a flour dough and butter, each layer being kept separate from the other, by trapped air.

Always use a good quality plain flour, and a good firm butter, one that is neither too oily, nor too wet. Getting the amount of water right is most important. The dough needs to be soft and elastic, without being sticky, yet firm enough to contain the butter without letting it break through.

When making puff pastry, it is essential to keep everything as cold as possible. The water should be well chilled, and the butter cold, but not so cold that it will be hard and break up, or break through the flour dough. Butter left at room temperature for about 15–20 minutes is usually just right by the time it has been beaten.

Puff pastry is best eaten on the day it is made, otherwise it firms up and loses the light, flaky texture it has when freshly baked.

---

225 g (8 oz) plain flour
pinch of salt
225 g (8 oz) slightly salted
  butter

15 ml (1 tbsp) strained
  lemon juice
a little less than 150 ml
  (¼ pint) iced water

Sift the flour and salt into a bowl. Lightly rub in 25 g (1 oz) of the butter.

Place the remaining butter between two sheets of clingfilm and beat it out firmly with a rolling pin to form a smooth 15 cm (6 inch) square, then set aside.

Make a well in the centre of the flour, add the lemon juice and iced water, then mix with a round-bladed knife to form a fairly soft, but not sticky dough. Place the dough on a lightly floured marble slab, or work surface, and, without kneading, roll out the dough to about a 25 cm (10 inch) square.

Place the square of butter in the centre of the dough, so that it looks like a diamond shape. Bring each corner of the dough to the centre of the butter, to enclose it completely, then turn the pastry 45 degrees to square it up.

Roll out the pastry to about 45.5 cm (18 inches) long, then take the bottom third of the pastry up and over the centre third, bring the top third of the pastry down over the bottom third, trapping in as much air as you can between each layer as you do so. Press the edges firmly with the rolling pin to seal. Wrap the pastry in clingfilm, put it on a plate and chill for 30 minutes. Do not leave the pastry in the refrigerator any longer than 30 minutes, this will harden the butter and cause it to break up when you roll the pastry out again.

Remove the clingfilm. Place the pastry on a lightly floured surface so that the short joined ends are at the top and the bottom. Roll out the pastry again to about 45.5 cm (18 inches) long. Fold into three once again, and seal. Brush off excess flour, then wrap and chill for another 30 minutes. Repeat this rolling out, and folding, process six more times, with a 30 minute rest between each one.

After the last folding and 30 minute rest, the pastry is ready to be used. Or, it may be wrapped in clean clingfilm, then in aluminium foil and be refrigerated for up to 3 days before using, or be frozen for up to 3 months.

Danish Pastry

Danish pastry, for making those celebrated Danish pastries, is made with a yeast dough enriched with butter, in a fashion very similar to puff pastry. The addition of yeast to the dough makes the pastry very light. The pastry does not require as many rollings and folding as does puff pastry, but all the basic rules for making puff pastry also apply to making Danish pastry.

275 g (10 oz) plain flour
pinch of salt
15 ml (1 tbsp) caster sugar
225 g (8 oz) butter, at
   room temperature
15 g (½ oz) fresh yeast or
   7.5 ml (1½ tsp) dried
   yeast and 5 ml (1 tsp)
   caster sugar

100 ml (4 fl oz) cold water
   (tepid if using dried
   yeast)
1 egg, beaten

MAKES EIGHTEEN PASTRIES

Sift the flour, salt and caster sugar into a bowl, then rub in 25 g (1 oz) of the butter. Blend the yeast and water; if using dried yeast add 5 ml (1 tsp) sugar.

Make a well in the centre of the flour, add the yeast liquid and the egg. Mix to form a soft dough, then knead lightly on a floured surface for about 5 minutes until smooth. Put the dough inside a very lightly oiled polythene bag and chill for 10 minutes.

Meanwhile, place the remaining butter between two sheets of greaseproof paper, or clingfilm, and beat out firmly with a rolling pin to form a 15 cm (6 inch) square.

Remove the dough from the polythene bag and roll it out to about a 25 cm (10 inch) square. Place the square of butter in the centre of the dough, so that it looks like a diamond shape, bring each corner of the dough to the centre of the butter, enclosing it completely.

Turn the dough 45 degrees to square it up, then roll out the pastry to about 45.5 cm (18 inches) long, take the bottom third of the pastry up and over the centre third, then bring the top third of the pastry down over the bottom third. Press all the edges firmly with the rolling pin to seal. Put the pastry inside a lightly oiled polythene bag and chill for 10 minutes. Turning the pastry so that the short ends are at the top and bottom each time, repeat the rolling out, and folding into three, three more times with a 10 minute rest in between each one. Use as required.

The pastry will keep for 2–3 days in the refrigerator.

Choux Pastry

This light, airy pastry is used for many classic gateaux, such as Croquembouche, Paris-Brest, and Gâteau Saint-Honoré. Due to the vast amount of air beaten into the pastry, it rises to four or five times its original size during baking, forming a hollow interior which is perfect for filling with flavoured whipped creams, or crème pâtissière.

The secret of making light, crispy, pastry is to take great care and not be too hasty when adding the beaten eggs. Thorough beating between each addition will ensure perfect results.

Choux pastry can be made very successfully by hand, but it is easier with a hand held electric mixer, or a large electric mixer.

125 g (4 oz) plain flour	225 ml (8 fl oz) cold water
pinch of salt	3 eggs, beaten
90 g (3½ oz) unsalted butter	

Sift the flour and the salt on to a small sheet of greaseproof paper. Put the butter and water in a saucepan, heat very gently until the butter melts. Bring to a rolling boil. (Do not allow the water to boil before the butter melts, as this will evaporate off some of the water, and will in turn reduce the amount of liquid.)

Remove the pan from the heat and tip the flour into the boiling liquid, stirring it into the liquid as you do so. Return the pan to the heat, then beat the mixture just until it forms a ball, and leaves the sides of the pan; do not overbeat as the paste will become oily and separate.

Remove the pan from the heat and allow the paste to cool a little. Pour a little of the beaten eggs into the pan, then beat them into the paste. Continue to add the eggs, a little at a time, beating well between each addition, until they are all incorporated, and you have a very smooth shiny paste. Use and bake as directed in the individual recipes.

Pâte Sucrée

This is a very rich, sweet pastry, sometimes called biscuit crust because of its biscuit-like texture. It is used mainly for making flan and tartlet cases. Because it has a high proportion of butter and sugar, it is a much softer pastry to use. In warm weather, it is best to chill it for half an hour before using.

Traditionally, this pastry is made directly on a marble slab – the flour being sifted on to the slab and a well made in the centre, into which are put the sugar, butter and egg yolks. The ingredients are then all gently worked together with the fingertips. However, equally good results are achieved by making the pastry in a mixing bowl, in the same way as rich shortcrust pastry. Use butter to ensure a good flavour.

150 g (5 oz) plain flour
pinch of salt
25 g (1 oz) icing sugar

75 g (3 oz) butter, cubed
2 egg yolks

MAKES ABOUT 275 g (10 oz)

Sift the flour, salt and icing sugar into a bowl. Rub in the butter until the mixture resembles fine breadcrumbs. Add the egg yolks and mix with a round-bladed knife to form a dough. Turn on to a lightly floured surface and knead for a few seconds until smooth.

Almond Pastry

Almond pastry is very similar to pâte sucrée, and is also used for flan and tartlet cases. Because it has the addition of ground almonds it is a very soft pastry to handle and must be chilled before using.

150 g (5 oz) plain flour
pinch of salt
40 g (1½ oz) caster sugar
50 g (2 oz) ground
almonds

90 g (3½ oz) butter, cubed
few drops of vanilla
essence
1 medium-sized egg,
beaten

MAKES ABOUT 400 g (14 oz)

Sift the flour, salt and sugar into a bowl, then mix in the ground almonds. Rub in the butter until the mixture resembles fine breadcrumbs. Make a well in the centre, add the vanilla and the beaten egg. Mix together with a round-bladed knife to form a dough. Turn on to a lightly floured surface and knead for a few seconds until smooth. Wrap the pastry in clingfilm and chill for 30–40 minutes until firm, before using.

Crème Pâtissière

A rich, thick, custard used as a filling for cakes, small pastries, and flans. Its light, smooth, cool texture contrasts and complements both sponge cakes and pastries alike. The basic mixture is flavoured with vanilla, but it can also be flavoured with liqueurs, chocolate, coffee, orange, or lemon rind.

Add liqueurs, such as Grand Marnier, Kirsch or brandy to the cold custard, but don't add too much or the custard will become thin. Chocolate, coffee, orange, or lemon rind should be heated with the milk.

It is always best to make the custard the day before it is to be used, to ensure that it is thoroughly chilled; for a firmer setting, a little gelatine can be added – where required, this is indicated in the recipes.

3 egg yolks	5 ml (1 tsp) vanilla
50 g (2 oz) caster sugar	essence
35 g (1¼ oz) plain flour,	1 egg white
sifted	150 ml (¼ pint) double
300 ml (½ pint) milk	cream

Whisk the egg yolks and 15 g (½ oz) caster sugar in a bowl until pale and thick. Fold in the flour.

Put the milk and the vanilla into a saucepan and bring almost to the boil. Gently whisk the hot milk into the egg and flour mixture. Strain the mixture, through a nylon sieve, back into the pan.

Cook the custard over a gentle heat, stirring, until the mixture thickens. Pour the hot custard into a clean bowl, then cover the surface closely with clingfilm to prevent a skin forming. Allow the custard to cool completely, but not to set too firmly.

Whisk the egg white until stiff, then gradually whisk in the remaining caster sugar. Whip the cream until thick.

Whisk the cooled custard until smooth, gradually fold in the egg white then the cream. Cover the crème pâtissière with clingfilm and thoroughly chill before using.

Crème Chantilly

The addition of sugar and vanilla essence before whipping, turns double cream into crème Chantilly, making the cream smoother and more flavourful. It is used extensively for filling and decorating cakes, large and small pastries, and desserts.

300 ml (½ pint) very fresh double cream, well chilled

15 ml (1 tbsp) icing sugar, sifted

2.5–5 ml (½–1 tsp) vanilla essence

Put the cream into a well chilled bowl with the sugar and vanilla essence to taste, then whip until the cream forms soft peaks, or a little thicker if required for piping. Take care not to overwhip the cream or it will turn buttery and be unusable.

Apricot Glaze

Apricot glaze is used for glazing pastries and flans to make them look more attractive; the addition of a little Kirsch or Grand Marnier gives extra flavour.
If using home-made jam add a little water; most brought jams are already quite thin and will melt down very easily but do use a good quality conserve rather than ordinary jam for the best taste. Raspberry and strawberry conserves can be used in exactly the same way to make a red glaze.

350 g (12 oz) jar apricot conserve

15–30 ml (1–2 tbsp) Kirsch, optional

Put the conserve into a small saucepan and heat gently, stirring all the time, until melted. Sieve the conserve through a nylon sieve into another small clean saucepan. Add the Kirsch, then bring to the boil, stirring. The glaze should always be at boiling point when used to ensure that it sets well.

Apricot glaze will keep well, stored in an airtight jar in a cool place, ready to be heated when required for glazing.

Index

A

Almonds:
Almond crescents 27
Almond pastry 92
Pithiviers 11
Angostura pie 54–5
Apples:
Fall compote 33
Flambéed apples 43
French apple tart 50–1
Old-fashioned apple pie 55
Swiss tart 80
Tray-bake tarts 54
Apricots:
Apricot envelopes 27–8
Apricot tart 50
Apricot glaze 94
Apricot soufflé with apricot sauce 59
Summer compote 32–3

B

Bavarois:
Strawberry bavarois 74–5
Vanilla Bavarian ring 74
Biscuit de Savoie 87
Blackberry mousse 71
Black currant fool 42
Black Forest cherry cake 14–15
Blueberry fool 42

C

Caramel crème 73
Cherries:
Black Forest cherry cake 14–15
Summer compote 32
Chestnut purée:
Meringue nests 84
Chocolate:
Chocolate and orange mousse 68
Chocolate crème 73
Chocolate éclairs 12
Meringue and ganache cake 82
Rigo Jansci 28
Sachertorte 23
Steamed chocolate soufflé with chocolate sauce 58
Choux pastry 91
Coeurs à la crème 72
Coffee:
Religieuse 13
Whisky mocha flan 52
Compotes, fruit 32–3
Cranberries:
Meringue nests 84
Cream, whipping 64–6
Crème brûlée 70
Crème Chantilly 94
Crème pâtissière 93
Croquembouche 30–1
Custard, making 64

D

Danish pastries 27–8,90
Dobostorte 24–6

E

Eclairs, chocolate 12
Egg whites, whisking 66

F

Flambéed apples 43
Flans 46–47, 50–52, 80
Fools, fruit 42
Fruit (*see* Apples *etc*):
Fresh fruit purées 43
Fresh fruit salad 40
Fresh fruit tartlets 48
Fruit compotes 32–3
Fruit fools 42
German rumtopf 36
Summer pudding 38–39

G

Gâteau Saint-Honoré 18–19
Gelatine 66
Génoise sponge 86–7
Glaze, apricot 94

H

Hazelnuts:
Hazelnut meringue cake 82–3
Nusskuchen 26
Pistachio and hazelnut galette 19

J

Jalousie 18
Jellies 42

K

Kumquats:
Winter compote 33

L

Lemon:
Lemon meringue pie 79
Salzburger Nockerln 63
Simple lemon soufflé 68
Lime:
Lime syllabub 72
Linzertorte 10
Loganberry sauce 44

M

Mangoes:
Mango and passion fruit sherbet 34
Tropical Pavlova 83
Melon and figs steeped in brandy 40
Meringues 76
Hazelnut meringue cake 82–3
Lemon meringue pie 79
Meringue and ganache cake 82
Meringue medley 78
Meringue nests 84
Swiss flan 80
Mille-feuille 12–13
Molds 66–7
Mousses 64, 68, 71, 72–3

N

Nusskuchen 26

O
Old English syllabub 71
Omelets, soufflé 57
Oranges:
  Chocolate and orange mousse 68
  Citrus mousse 72–3
  Orange and Grand Marnier
    soufflé 60
  Oranges cooked in caramel 38

P
Palmiers 22
Paris-Brest 15
Passion fruit and mango sorbet 34
Passion fruit soufflé 67
Pastry 88–92
Pâte sucrée 92
Pavlova, tropical 83
Peaches:
  Peaches with loganberry sauce 44
  Summer compote 32–3
Pears:
  Autumn compote 33
  Pears cooked in red wine 39
Pies 46–7, 54–5
Pineapple sorbet 35
Pinwheels, spiced 26–7
Pistachio and hazelnut galette 16
Pistachio fingers 79

Pithiviers 11
Plums:
  Fall compote 33
Puff pastry 89

R
Raspberries:
  Hazelnut meringue cake 82–3
  Jalousie 16
  Raspberry sherbet 34
  Raspberry soufflés 63, 70
  Raspberry torte 20–2
Religieuse 13
Rhubarb:
  Spring compote 32
Rigo Jancsi 28
Rumtopf, German 36

S
Sachertorte 23
Salzburger Nockerln 63
Schwarzwalder Kirschtorte 14–15
Sherbets 34
Shortcrust pastry 88
Soufflé omelets 57
Soufflé crêpes with blackberry
    sauce 62
Soufflés:
  baked 56–7, 59–60, 63
  cold 64, 67–70

dishes for 66–7
  steamed 57, 58
Sponge cakes 86–7
Strawberries:
  Palmiers 22
  Strawberry and loganberry gelatin 42
  Strawberry Bavarois 74–5
  Strawberry tart 51
Summer pudding 38–39
Swiss tart 80
Syllabubs:
  Lime syllabub 72
  Old English syllabub 71

T
Tartlets, fresh fruit 48
Tarts 46–7, 54
Tropical Pavlova 83

V
Vanilla:
  Crème brûlée 70
  Crème Chantilly 94
  Crème pâtissière 93
  Vanilla Bavarian ring 74
  Vanilla soufflé 59–60

W
Whiskey mocha flan 52

THE NEW HARTFORD MEMORIAL LIBRARY
P.O. Box 247
Central Avenue at Town Hill Road
New Hartford, Connecticut 06057
(860) 379-7235